RSC School Shakespeare

T0351894

Series consultant: Emma Smith
Professor of Shakespeare Studies
Hertford College, University of Oxford

THE TEMPEST

OXFORD

UNIVERSITY PRESS

OXFORD
UNIVERSITY PRESS

Great Clarendon Street, Oxford, OX2 6DP,
United Kingdom

Oxford University Press is a department of the University of Oxford.
It furthers the University's objective of excellence in research, scholarship,
and education by publishing worldwide. Oxford is a registered trade mark of Oxford
University Press in the UK and in certain other countries

First published in 2018

British Library Cataloguing in Publication Data

Data available

ISBN 978-019-836482-5

10 9 8 7 6 5

Printed in Great Britain by Ashford Colour Press Ltd.

Acknowledgements

We are indebted to all of those teachers and practitioners who have contributed to
the development of the work in this series. In particular Cicely Berry whose work is a
constant source of inspiration. The material in these editions was primarily written by
RSC Education Associate Practitioners Tracy Irish and Rachel Gartside but we also wish to
acknowledge the contributions of Mary Johnson and Miles Tandy. Editorial work for the
RSC was undertaken by Jacqui O'Hanlon.

Cover and performance images © Royal Shakespeare Company 2018

Cover image by Ellie Kurttz. Other The Tempest performance images by Manuel Harlan
(2006), Ellie Kurttz (2009), Simon Annand (2012) and Topher McGrillis (2016, 2017)

p182(t): © Corbis/Getty Images; p182(m): Shutterstock; p182(b): Shutterstock; p183(t):
19th era/Alamy Stock Photo; p183(mt): Granger Historical Picture Archive/Alamy Stock
Photo; p183(mb): © National Portrait Gallery, London; p183(b): Royal Shakespeare
Company Theatre Collection; p186: DEA PICTURE LIBRARY/Getty Images; p187: Hulton
Archive/Getty Images; p186: Royal Shakespeare Company Theatre Collection; p189:
Gimas/Shutterstock.

Layout by Justin Hoffmann at Pixelfox

Contents

Introduction to *RSC School Shakespeare* 4

    The RSC approach 4
    Using *RSC School Shakespeare* 6

Introducing *The Tempest* 8

    The play in performance 8
    The play at a glance 10

The Tempest 15

    Act 1 17
        Exploring Act 1 60
    Act 2 63
        Exploring Act 2 98
    Act 3 101
        Exploring Act 3 128
    Act 4 131
        Exploring Act 4 150
    Act 5 153
        Exploring Act 5 178
        Exploring the play 180

William Shakespeare and his world 182

    Shakespeare's life 182
    Shakespeare's language 184
    Shakespeare's world 186

Key terms glossary 198

The RSC approach

The classroom as rehearsal room

All the work of RSC Education is underpinned by the artistic practice of the Royal Shakespeare Company (RSC). In particular, we make very strong connections between the rehearsal rooms in which our actors and directors work and the classrooms in which you learn. Rehearsal rooms are essentially places of exploration and shared discovery, in which a company of actors and their director work together to bring Shakespeare's plays to life. To do this successfully they need to have a deep understanding of the text, to get the language 'in the body' and to be open to a range of interpretive possibilities and choices. The ways in which they do this are both active and playful, connecting mind, voice and body.

Becoming a company

To do this we begin by deliberately building a spirit of one group with a shared purpose – this is about 'us' rather than 'me'. We often do this with games that warm up our brains, voices and bodies, and we continue to build this spirit through a scheme of work that includes shared, collaborative tasks that depend on and value everyone's contributions. The ways in which the activities work in this edition encourage discussion, speculation and questioning: there is rarely one right answer. This process requires and develops critical thinking.

Making the world of the play

In rehearsals at the RSC, we explore the whole world of the play: we tackle the language, characters and motivation, setting, plot and themes. By 'standing in the shoes' of the characters and exploring the world of the play, you will be engaged fully: head, eyes, ears, hands, bodies and hearts are involved in actively interpreting the play. In grappling with scenes and speeches, you are also actively grappling with the themes and ideas in the play, experiencing them from the points of view of the different characters.

RSC rehearsal

The language is central to our discoveries

We place the language in the plays at the core of everything we do. Active, playful approaches can make Shakespeare's words vivid, accessible and enjoyable. His language has the power to excite and delight all of us.

In the rehearsal room, the RSC uses social and historical context in order to deepen understanding of the world of the play. The company is engaged in a 'conversation across time', inviting audiences to consider what a play means to us now and what it meant to us then. We hope that the activities in this edition will offer you an opportunity to join that conversation.

The activities require close, critical reading and encourage you to make informed interpretive choices about language, character and motivation, themes and plot. The work is rooted in speaking and listening to Shakespeare's words and to each other's ideas in order to help embrace and unlock this extraordinary literary inheritance.

Jacqui O'Hanlon
Director of Education
Royal Shakespeare Company

The Royal Shakespeare Theatre

Using *RSC School Shakespeare*

As you open each double page, you will see the script of the play on the right-hand page. On the left-hand page is a series of features that will help you connect with and explore William Shakespeare's play *The Tempest* and the world in which Shakespeare lived.

Those features are:

Summary

At the top of every left-hand page is a summary of what happens on the facing page to help you understand the action.

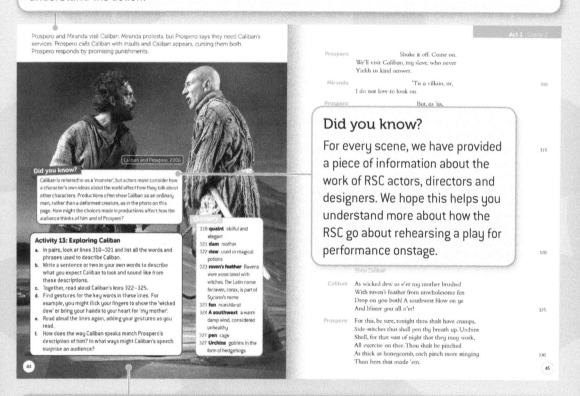

Prospero and Miranda visit Caliban. Miranda protests, but Prospero says they need Caliban's services. Prospero calls Caliban with insults and Caliban appears, cursing them both. Prospero responds by promising punishments.

Caliban and Prospero, 2006

Did you know?

Caliban is referred to as a 'monster', but actors must consider how a character's own ideas about the world affect how they talk about other characters. Productions often show Caliban as an ordinary man, rather than a deformed creature, as in the photo on this page. How might the choices made in productions affect how the audience thinks of him and of Prospero?

Glossary

318 **quaint** skilful and elegant
321 **dam** mother
322 **dew** used in magical potions
323 **raven's feather** Ravens were associated with witches. The Latin name for raven, corax, is part of Sycorax's name
323 **fen** marshland
324 **A southwest** a warm damp wind, considered unhealthy
327 **pen** cage
327 **Urchins** goblins in the form of hedgehogs

Activity 13: Exploring Caliban

a. In pairs, look at lines 310–321 and list all the words and phrases used to describe Caliban.
b. Write a sentence or two in your own words to describe what you expect Caliban to look and sound like from these descriptions.
c. Together, read aloud Caliban's lines 322–325.
d. Find gestures for the key words in these lines. For example, you might flick your fingers to show the 'wicked dew' or bring your hands to your heart for 'my mother'.
e. Read aloud the lines again, adding your gestures as you read.
f. How does the way Caliban speaks match Prospero's description of him? In what ways might Caliban's speech surprise an audience?

44

Act 1 | Scene 2

Prospero	Shake it off. Come on. We'll visit Caliban, my slave, who never Yields us kind answer.	
Miranda	'Tis a villain, sir, I do not love to look on.	310
Prospero	But, as 'tis,	

Did you know?

For every scene, we have provided a piece of information about the work of RSC actors, directors and designers. We hope this helps you understand more about how the RSC go about rehearsing a play for performance onstage.

315

Enter Caliban

| Caliban | As wicked dew as e'er my mother brushed With raven's feather from unwholesome fen Drop on you both! A southwest blow on ye And blister you all o'er! | 325 |
| Prospero | For this, be sure, tonight thou shalt have cramps, Side-stitches that shall pen thy breath up. Urchins Shall, for that vast of night that they may work, All exercise on thee. Thou shalt be pinched As thick as honeycomb, each pinch more stinging Than bees that made 'em. | 330 |

45

320

RSC performance photographs

Every left-hand page includes at least one photograph from an RSC production of the play. Some of the activities make direct use of the production photographs. The photographs illustrate the action, bringing to life the text on the facing page. They also include a caption that identifies the character or event, together with the date of the RSC production.

Glossary

Where needed, there is a glossary that explains words from the play that may be unfamiliar and cannot be worked out in context.

At the time

There are social and historical research tasks, so that you can use knowledge from the time the play was written to help you interpret the text of the play. The social and historical information can be found on pages 182–197 of this edition.

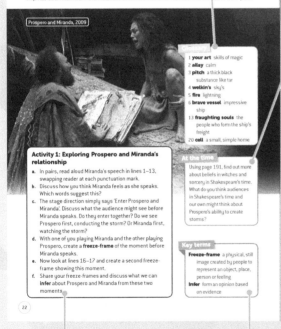

Miranda is distressed at watching a ship wrecked offshore and believes her father Prospero has created the storm using his magical powers. Prospero assures her that no one on the ship has been harmed. He announces that it is time for her to know more about their past.

Prospero and Miranda, 2009

1 **your art** skills of magic
2 **allay** calm
3 **pitch** a thick black substance like tar
4 **welkin's** sky's
5 **fire** lightning
6 **brave vessel** impressive ship
13 **fraughting souls** the people who form the ship's freight
20 **cell** a small, simple home

Activity 1: Exploring Prospero and Miranda's relationship

a. In pairs, read aloud Miranda's speech in lines 1–13, swapping reader at each punctuation mark.
b. Discuss how you think Miranda feels as she speaks. Which words suggest this?
c. The stage direction simply says 'Enter Prospero and Miranda'. Discuss what the audience might see before Miranda speaks. Do they enter together? Do we see Prospero first, conducting the storm? Or Miranda first, watching the storm?
d. With one of you playing Miranda and the other playing Prospero, create a **freeze-frame** of the moment before Miranda speaks.
e. Now look at lines 16–17 and create a second freeze-frame showing this moment.
f. Share your freeze-frames and discuss what we can **infer** about Prospero and Miranda from these two moments.

At the time

Using page 191, find out more about beliefs in witches and sorcery in Shakespeare's time. What do you think audiences in Shakespeare's time and our own might think about Prospero's ability to create storms?

Key terms

Freeze-frame a physical, still image created by people to represent an object, place, person or feeling
Infer form an opinion based on evidence

22

Act 1 | Scene 2

Enter Prospero and Miranda

Miranda   If by your art, my dearest father, you have
Put the wild waters in this roar, allay them.
The sky, it seems, would pour down stinking pitch,
But that the sea, mounting to the welkin's cheek,
Dashes the fire out. O, I have suffered   5
With those that I saw suffer! A brave vessel,
Who had, no doubt, some noble creature in her,
Dashed all to pieces. O, the cry did knock
Against my very heart! Poor souls, they perished.
Had I been any god of power, I would   10
Have sunk the sea within the earth or ere
It should the good ship so have swallowed, and
The fraughting souls within her.

Prospero   Be collected.
No more amazement. Tell your piteous heart
There's no harm done.

Miranda   O, woe the day!

Prospero   No harm.   15
I have done nothing but in care of thee,
Of thee, my dear one, thee, my daughter, who
Art ignorant of what thou art, nought knowing
Of whence I am, nor that I am more better
Than Prospero, master of a full poor cell,   20
And thy no greater father.

Miranda   More to know
Did never meddle with my thoughts.

Prospero   'Tis time
I should inform thee farther. Lend thy hand

23

Activity

Every left-hand page includes at least one activity that is inspired by RSC rehearsal room practice.

Key terms

Where needed, there is an explanation of any key terms used, literary or theatrical.

The play in performance

Shakespeare's last play

The Tempest is the last complete play solely attributed to Shakespeare. It was presented at court for King James I on 1 November 1611. The play formed part of the festivities for the marriage of King James' daughter, Princess Elizabeth, to Prince Frederick (later King of Bohemia). It would have been unusual to risk a play's first ever performance before the king and so it is safe to assume that *The Tempest* had already been performed in public.

At the Royal Shakespeare Company (RSC), we have staged countless productions of *The Tempest* and each time they are completely different. Shakespeare's plays are packed full of questions and challenges for the director, designer and acting company to solve. The clues to finding the answers are always somewhere in the text, but the possibilities for interpretation are infinite.

Ferdinand and Miranda, 2016

A place of possibilities

The Tempest is a really exciting play to work on but it also presents some real challenges for the director and actors tasked with bringing it to life on stage.

One of the most interesting challenges faced by a director in bringing *The Tempest* to life on stage is how to deal with the mystical nature of the island. Ariel is neither male or female – or is both. Caliban is the son of a witch. And the island is populated with spirits who take on different forms. In one RSC production, the island became an arctic wilderness, in others a tropical paradise. The director and designer work together to develop a world in which all the characters in the play can meet and interact. Actors and their director then try out different ways of playing scenes informed always by the clues that Shakespeare gives them; they effectively become text detectives, mining the language for clues to help inform their performance choices.

Ariel, 2009

We have taken all of the ways of working of our actors and directors and set them alongside the text of *The Tempest* which, together with the other titles in the series, offers a great introduction to Shakespeare's world and work. An actor once described the rehearsal room to me as a 'place of possibilities'. I think that's a wonderful way of thinking about a classroom too and it's what we hope the RSC School Shakespeare editions help to create.

Jacqui O'Hanlon
Director of Education
Royal Shakespeare Company

The play at a glance

Every scene in a play presents a challenge to the actors and their director in terms of how to stage it. There are certain key moments in a play that directors need to pay special attention to because they contain really significant events.

The scene is set (Act 1 Scene 1)

There is a huge storm at sea. King Alonso of Naples is on a ship with his son, Prince Ferdinand. The king's brother, Sebastian, and his advisor, Gonzalo, Duke Antonio, a butler, Stephano, and a jester, Trinculo, all expect to drown.

The island (Act 1 Scene 2)

From a nearby island Miranda watches the huge tempest. She is fifteen and has never known anything other than this isolated life. She lives with her father, Prospero. He has studied magic and can conjure up various forces. Prospero is helped by his spirit, Ariel, and a slave, Caliban, who is the son of an old witch, Sycorax.

Miranda cries as she watches the shipwreck. She begs her father to calm the storm that he has created. He reassures her that it will calm down now. No one will be harmed; King Alonso and the crew will arrive

Prospero and Miranda, 2016

on the island. Ariel helped Prospero to make the storm and he asks for his freedom in return. Prospero refuses and reminds Ariel how he rescued him from the trunk of a pine tree where the witch Sycorax had left him encased. Prospero will free him in just two days.

Prospero tells Miranda of their past. He was the Duke of Milan just twelve years ago. But he was so involved with his books and secret studies that he did not realise that his brother, Antonio, was stealing power from him. King Alonso and Antonio plotted together against Prospero. Hired soldiers dragged Miranda and Prospero from their home. They were put out to sea in a small rotten boat and left to die. They were given food and water by Gonzalo who pitied them.

Prince Ferdinand enters and he and Miranda fall instantly in love.

Ferdinand, Prospero and Miranda, 2009

Stephano and Caliban, 2006

Antonio's plan (Act 2 Scene 1)

The shipwrecked crew wander round the island amazed, searching for each other. King Alonso mourns for his son Ferdinand who he fears is dead. Antonio convinces Sebastian to try to kill the king so that Sebastian can rule Naples. They also plot to kill Gonzalo.

A new master (Act 2 Scene 2)

Stephano and Trinculo are two members of the shipwrecked crew, who have been separated. Stephano drinks a lot. Caliban and Trinculo shelter from the rain under a cloak. Stephano sees them and believes they are a four-legged monster. Stephano gives them wine and because of this, Caliban offers to serve Stephano as his new master, instead of Prospero.

A proposal (Act 3 Scene 1)

Prospero wants Miranda and Ferdinand to be together but tests their love first. He makes Ferdinand chop and carry endless logs. Miranda is tormented by her father's treatment of him and pities the prince. Miranda proposes marriage and Ferdinand willingly agrees.

The attempted attack (Act 4 Scene 1)

Trinculo, Stephano and Caliban prepare to attack Prospero, but he and Ariel are prepared and send sprites and spirit dogs to hound and chase them away.

Reunited (Act 5 Scene 1)

The king's party meet Prospero who shows them Ferdinand and Miranda playing chess. He thanks Gonzalo for helping them twelve years ago when they were exiled and announces the love between Miranda and Ferdinand. King Alonso is sorry for his actions. Prospero forgives him. The young lovers will be married and Prospero will be reinstated in Milan.

Miranda is amazed and enchanted by seeing so many people. Ariel has been aching for his freedom and Prospero lets him go now. Prospero gives up his magic powers and prepares to leave the island and travel to Naples.

Alonso, Ferdinand, Sebastian, Miranda and Prospero, 2016

The Tempest

The inhabitants of the island

Prospero, the former Duke of Milan, now living on the island
Miranda, Prospero's daughter, living with him
Caliban, born on the island, serves Prospero
Ariel, chief spirit of the island, serves Prospero

Spirits of the island who play the roles of:

Iris
Ceres
Juno
Nymphs
Reapers

The King's company, shipwrecked on the island

Alonso, King of Naples
Ferdinand, Alonso's son
Sebastian, Alonso's brother
Antonio, Prospero's brother, the current Duke of Milan
Gonzalo, Alonso's councillor
Adrian & Francisco, lords, loyal to Alonso
Trinculo, Alonso's jester
Stephano, Alonso's butler
Master of the ship
Boatswain
Mariners

A ship carrying Alonso the King of Naples, his son Ferdinand, Antonio the Duke of Milan, and other companions is caught in a violent storm. The crew are trying to steer her to safety while the king's companions get in the way.

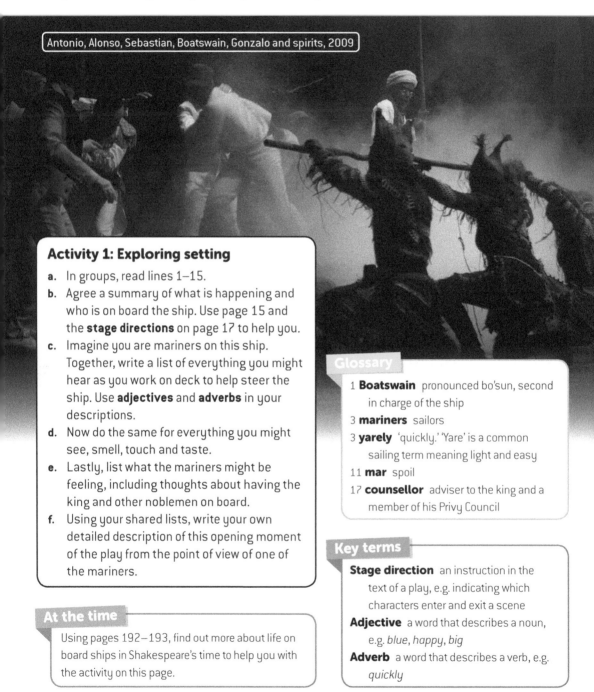

Antonio, Alonso, Sebastian, Boatswain, Gonzalo and spirits, 2009

Activity 1: Exploring setting

a. In groups, read lines 1–15.

b. Agree a summary of what is happening and who is on board the ship. Use page 15 and the **stage directions** on page 17 to help you.

c. Imagine you are mariners on this ship. Together, write a list of everything you might hear as you work on deck to help steer the ship. Use **adjectives** and **adverbs** in your descriptions.

d. Now do the same for everything you might see, smell, touch and taste.

e. Lastly, list what the mariners might be feeling, including thoughts about having the king and other noblemen on board.

f. Using your shared lists, write your own detailed description of this opening moment of the play from the point of view of one of the mariners.

Glossary

1 **Boatswain** pronounced bo'sun, second in charge of the ship

3 **mariners** sailors

3 **yarely** 'quickly.' 'Yare' is a common sailing term meaning light and easy

11 **mar** spoil

17 **counsellor** adviser to the king and a member of his Privy Council

Key terms

Stage direction an instruction in the text of a play, e.g. indicating which characters enter and exit a scene

Adjective a word that describes a noun, e.g. *blue*, *happy*, *big*

Adverb a word that describes a verb, e.g. *quickly*

At the time

Using pages 192–193, find out more about life on board ships in Shakespeare's time to help you with the activity on this page.

Act 1 | Scene 1

A tempestuous noise of thunder and lightning heard. Enter a Shipmaster and a Boatswain

Master   Boatswain!

Boatswain   Here, master. What cheer?

Master   Good. Speak to the mariners. Fall to it yarely, or we run ourselves aground! Bestir, bestir!

Exit Master. Enter Mariners

Boatswain   Heigh, my hearts! Cheerly, cheerly, my hearts! Yare, yare! Take in   5
the topsail. Tend to the master's whistle. [To the storm] Blow, till
thou burst thy wind, if room enough.

Enter Alonso, Sebastian, Antonio, Ferdinand, Gonzalo and others

Alonso   Good boatswain, have care. Where's the master? Play the men.

Boatswain   I pray now, keep below.

Antonio   Where is the master, boatswain?   10

Boatswain   Do you not hear him? You mar our labour. Keep your cabins.
You do assist the storm.

Gonzalo   Nay, good, be patient.

Boatswain   When the sea is. Hence! What cares these roarers for the name of
king? To cabin! Silence! Trouble us not!   15

Gonzalo   Good, yet remember whom thou hast aboard.

Boatswain   None that I more love than myself. You are a counsellor, if you
can command these elements to silence, and work the peace of the
present, we will not hand a rope more. Use your authority. If you
cannot, give thanks you have lived so long, and make yourself   20
ready in your cabin for the mischance of the hour, if it so hap.

The nobles argue with the Boatswain as he shouts orders to his men. The mariners lose control of the ship and everyone fears the worst.

Alonso, Gonzalo, Ferdinand and Boatswain, 2016

Glossary

25 **drowning mark...** Gonzalo is referring to a proverb 'he that is born to be hanged shall never be drowned'. He thinks the Boatswain's lack of respect for authority figures means he will end up hanged

26 **the rope of his destiny** the hangman's noose

38 **warrant him for drowning** guarantee him against drowning

39 **unstanched wench** promiscuous or menstruating woman

Activity 2: Exploring the theme of authority and power

a. In pairs, read lines 14–23, swapping reader at each punctuation mark.

b. Discuss who has most power at this moment: the King of Naples, the Boatswain, Gonzalo, nature? Who has most authority?

c. What do you think are the similarities and differences between having power and having authority?

d. Now read lines 32–37, with one of you reading the Boatswain's lines and the other reading as Sebastian and Antonio.

e. Repeat task d, whispering your lines and emphasising each word.

f. Repeat again but this time speaking loudly to be heard above the storm.

g. Discuss whether any lines felt better whispered. What quality might whispering add to the exchange?

h. What does this exchange add to your thoughts about authority and power?

Key terms

Tone as in 'tone of voice'; expressing an attitude through how you say something

Pace the speed at which someone speaks

Emphasis stress given to words when speaking

Theme the main ideas explored in a piece of literature, e.g. the themes of power and authority, hope and fear, family, vengeance and forgiveness might be considered key themes of The Tempest

[To the Mariners] Cheerly, good hearts! [To the others] Out of our way, I say!

Exit Boatswain and Mariners

Gonzalo   I have great comfort from this fellow. Methinks he hath no drowning mark upon him – his complexion is perfect gallows!   25
Stand fast, good Fate, to his hanging. Make the rope of his destiny our cable, for our own doth little advantage. If he be not born to be hanged, our case is miserable.

Exeunt Gonzalo with Alonso, Sebastian, Antonio and Ferdinand

Enter Boatswain

Boatswain   Down with the topmast! Yare! Lower, lower! Bring her to try with main course. [A cry within] A plague upon this howling! They are   30
louder than the weather or our office.

Enter Sebastian, Antonio and Gonzalo

Yet again? What do you here? Shall we give o'er and drown? Have you a mind to sink?

Sebastian   A pox o'your throat, you bawling, blasphemous, incharitable dog!

Boatswain   Work you then.   35

Antonio   Hang, cur! Hang, you whoreson, insolent noisemaker! We are less afraid to be drowned than thou art.

Gonzalo   I'll warrant him for drowning, though the ship were no stronger than a nutshell and as leaky as an unstanched wench.

Boatswain   Lay her ahold, ahold! Set her two courses off to sea again! Lay   40
her off!

Enter Mariners, wet

Mariners   All lost! To prayers, to prayers! All lost!

Boatswain   What, must our mouths be cold?

Gonzalo   The king and prince at prayers. Let's assist them,
For our case is as theirs.

Activity 3: Staging a tempest

a. Look at the photos on this page and on pages 16 and 18, all taken from three different RSC productions.

b. Discuss which design you think looks most effective in creating the **atmosphere** of the storm and why.

c. Discuss why you think Shakespeare decided to open the play with this scene. What effect might it have on an audience? What impression have you gained of the characters we meet? What questions do you have about these characters?

Glossary

47 **wide-chopped** loud-mouthed

56 **fain** rather

Key terms

Staging the process of selecting, adapting and developing the stage space in which a play will be performed

Atmosphere the mood created by staging choices

Mariner, Gonzalo, Boatswain and Sebastian, 2006

Sebastian	I'm out of patience.	45

Antonio We are merely cheated of our lives by drunkards.
This wide-chopped rascal – would thou mightst lie drowning,
The washing of ten tides!

Gonzalo   He'll be hanged yet,
Though every drop of water swear against it,
And gape at wid'st to glut him.

Exeunt Boatswain and Mariners. A confused noise within

Mariners   [Within] Mercy on us!   50
We split, we split! Farewell, my wife and children!
Farewell, brother! We split, we split, we split!

Antonio Let's all sink with the king.

Sebastian   Let's take leave of him.

Exeunt Antonio and Sebastian

Gonzalo Now would I give a thousand furlongs of sea for an acre of
barren ground, long heath, brown furze, anything. The wills above   55
be done, but I would fain die a dry death.

Exit

Miranda is distressed at watching a ship wrecked offshore and believes her father Prospero has created the storm using his magical powers. Prospero assures her that no one on the ship has been harmed. He announces that it is time for her to know more about their past.

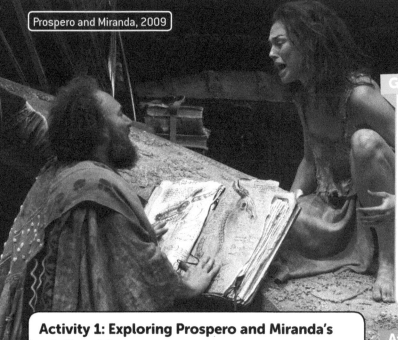

Prospero and Miranda, 2009

Glossary

1 **your art** skills of magic
2 **allay** calm
3 **pitch** a thick black substance like tar
4 **welkin's** sky's
5 **fire** lightning
6 **brave vessel** impressive ship
13 **fraughting souls** the people who form the ship's freight
20 **cell** a small, simple home

Activity 1: Exploring Prospero and Miranda's relationship

a. In pairs, read aloud Miranda's speech in lines 1–13, swapping reader at each punctuation mark.
b. Discuss how you think Miranda feels as she speaks. Which words suggest this?
c. The stage direction simply says 'Enter Prospero and Miranda'. Discuss what the audience might see before Miranda speaks. Do they enter together? Do we see Prospero first, conducting the storm? Or Miranda first, watching the storm?
d. With one of you playing Miranda and the other playing Prospero, create a **freeze-frame** of the moment before Miranda speaks.
e. Now look at lines 16–17 and create a second freeze-frame showing this moment.
f. Share your freeze-frames and discuss what we can **infer** about Prospero and Miranda from these two moments.

At the time

Using page 191, find out more about beliefs in witches and sorcery in Shakespeare's time. What do you think audiences in Shakespeare's time and our own might think about Prospero's ability to create storms?

Key terms

Freeze-frame a physical, still image created by people to represent an object, place, person or feeling
Infer form an opinion based on evidence

Enter Prospero and Miranda

Miranda   If by your art, my dearest father, you have
Put the wild waters in this roar, allay them.
The sky, it seems, would pour down stinking pitch,
But that the sea, mounting to the welkin's cheek,
Dashes the fire out. O, I have suffered   5
With those that I saw suffer! A brave vessel,
Who had, no doubt, some noble creature in her,
Dashed all to pieces. O, the cry did knock
Against my very heart! Poor souls, they perished.
Had I been any god of power, I would   10
Have sunk the sea within the earth or ere
It should the good ship so have swallowed, and
The fraughting souls within her.

Prospero   Be collected.
No more amazement. Tell your piteous heart
There's no harm done.

Miranda   O, woe the day!

Prospero   No harm.   15
I have done nothing but in care of thee,
Of thee, my dear one, thee, my daughter, who
Art ignorant of what thou art, nought knowing
Of whence I am, nor that I am more better
Than Prospero, master of a full poor cell,   20
And thy no greater father.

Miranda   More to know
Did never meddle with my thoughts.

Prospero   'Tis time
I should inform thee farther. Lend thy hand

Prospero again reassures Miranda that everyone on the ship is safe. He then asks if she can remember anything from before they arrived on the island when she was three years old. Miranda says she vaguely remembers four or five women who looked after her.

Prospero and Miranda, 2006

Key terms

Iambic pentameter the rhythm Shakespeare uses to write his plays. Each line in this rhythm contains approximately ten **syllables**. 'Iambic' means putting the stress on the second syllable of each beat. 'Pentameter' means five beats with two syllables in each beat

Syllable part of a word that is one sound, e.g. 'tempest' has two syllables 'tem' and 'pest'

Activity 2: Exploring rhythm

a. Read the description of **iambic pentameter** in the 'Key terms' box.
b. Say out loud: 'and ONE, and TWO, and THREE, and FOUR, and FIVE'.
c. Repeat and clap the rhythm as you speak. The rhythm is the same as the rhythm of your heartbeat.
d. Read aloud line 37 fitting the words to this rhythm.
e. In pairs, read aloud lines 28–37 with one of you reading as Prospero and the other as Miranda. Fit your reading to the iambic pentameter rhythm and notice how the characters take up each other's rhythm as they speak, sharing a line of iambic pentameter. Discuss what this might suggest about their relationship.
f. What does the photo on this page suggest about Prospero and Miranda's relationship?

Did you know?

Actors use the rhythm in Shakespeare's language to help them understand the script. Sometimes there are irregularities in the rhythm, which can indicate a character is disturbed or distracted. Sometimes characters share the rhythm, which can be a clue about how close they are or how urgent their conversation is.

And pluck my magic garment from me. So.

Miranda takes off his cloak

Lie there, my art. Wipe thou thine eyes, have comfort.   25
The direful spectacle of the wreck, which touched
The very virtue of compassion in thee,
I have with such provision in mine art
So safely ordered that there is no soul,
No, not so much perdition as an hair   30
Betid to any creature in the vessel
Which thou heard'st cry, which thou saw'st sink. Sit down.
For thou must now know farther.

Miranda   You have often
Begun to tell me what I am, but stopped
And left me to a bootless inquisition,   35
Concluding, 'Stay, not yet'.

Prospero   The hour's now come,
The very minute bids thee ope thine ear.
Obey, and be attentive. Canst thou remember
A time before we came unto this cell?
I do not think thou canst, for then thou wast not   40
Out three years old.

Miranda   Certainly, sir, I can.

Prospero   By what? By any other house or person?
Of any thing the image, tell me, that
Hath kept with thy remembrance.

Miranda   'Tis far off,
And rather like a dream than an assurance   45
That my remembrance warrants. Had I not
Four or five women once that tended me?

Prospero   Thou hadst, and more, Miranda. But how is it
That this lives in thy mind? What seest thou else
In the dark backward and abyss of time?   50
If thou rememb'rest aught ere thou cam'st here,

Prospero explains to Miranda that 12 years ago he was the powerful Duke of Milan. In order to spend more time on his studies, however, he had trusted his brother Antonio with the day-to-day running of his dukedom, but this was a mistake.

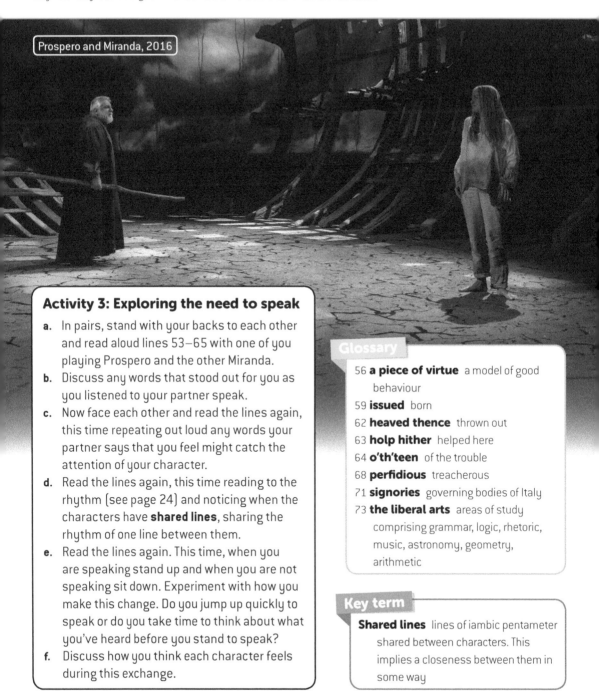

Prospero and Miranda, 2016

Activity 3: Exploring the need to speak

a. In pairs, stand with your backs to each other and read aloud lines 53–65 with one of you playing Prospero and the other Miranda.

b. Discuss any words that stood out for you as you listened to your partner speak.

c. Now face each other and read the lines again, this time repeating out loud any words your partner says that you feel might catch the attention of your character.

d. Read the lines again, this time reading to the rhythm (see page 24) and noticing when the characters have **shared lines**, sharing the rhythm of one line between them.

e. Read the lines again. This time, when you are speaking stand up and when you are not speaking sit down. Experiment with how you make this change. Do you jump up quickly to speak or do you take time to think about what you've heard before you stand to speak?

f. Discuss how you think each character feels during this exchange.

Key term

Shared lines lines of iambic pentameter shared between characters. This implies a closeness between them in some way

How thou cam'st here thou mayst.

Miranda   But that I do not.

Prospero Twelve year since, Miranda, twelve year since,
Thy father was the Duke of Milan and
A prince of power.

Miranda   Sir, are not you my father?   55

Prospero Thy mother was a piece of virtue, and
She said thou wast my daughter; and thy father
Was Duke of Milan, and his only heir
And princess, no worse issued.

Miranda   O the heavens!
What foul play had we, that we came from thence?   60
Or blessèd was't we did?

Prospero   Both, both, my girl.
By foul play, as thou say'st, were we heaved thence,
But blessedly holp hither.

Miranda   O, my heart bleeds
To think o'th'teen that I have turned you to,
Which is from my remembrance. Please you, farther.   65

Prospero My brother and thy uncle, called Antonio –
I pray thee, mark me – that a brother should
Be so perfidious – he whom next thyself
Of all the world I loved, and to him put
The manage of my state, as at that time   70
Through all the signories it was the first,
And Prospero the prime duke, being so reputed
In dignity, and for the liberal arts
Without a parallel; those being all my study,
The government I cast upon my brother   75
And to my state grew stranger, being transported
And rapt in secret studies. Thy false uncle –
Dost thou attend me?

Miranda   Sir, most heedfully.

Prospero tells Miranda how his brother Antonio abused his trust, manipulating the people of Milan to be loyal to him instead of Prospero and stealing all the power for himself.

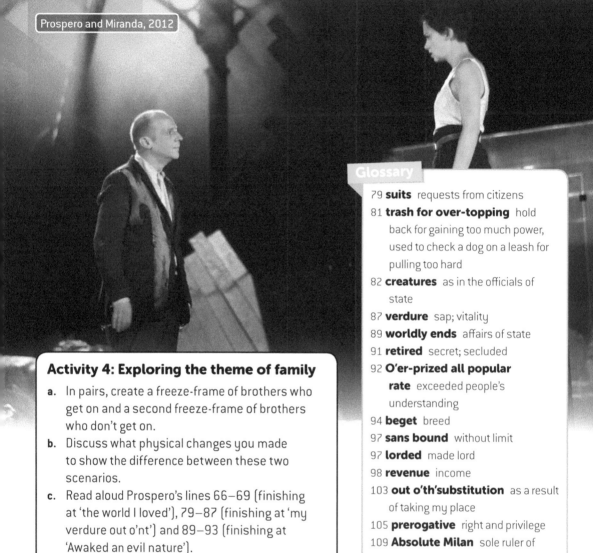

Prospero and Miranda, 2012

Activity 4: Exploring the theme of family

a. In pairs, create a freeze-frame of brothers who get on and a second freeze-frame of brothers who don't get on.

b. Discuss what physical changes you made to show the difference between these two scenarios.

c. Read aloud Prospero's lines 66–69 (finishing at 'the world I loved'), 79–87 (finishing at 'my verdure out o'nt') and 89–93 (finishing at 'Awaked an evil nature').

d. Discuss what you learn from these lines about Prospero's relationship with his brother. Which words or phrases particularly help you to understand their relationship?

e. Look again at lines 85–87. What does this **metaphor** suggest about how Prospero feels about his brother?

Key term

Metaphor describing something by comparing it with something else

Prospero	Being once perfected how to grant suits,	
	How to deny them, who t'advance and who	80
	To trash for over-topping, new created	
	The creatures that were mine, I say, or changed 'em,	
	Or else new formed 'em; having both the key	
	Of officer and office, set all hearts i'th'state	
	To what tune pleased his ear, that now he was	85
	The ivy which had hid my princely trunk	
	And sucked my verdure out on't. Thou attend'st not.	

Prospero   Being once perfected how to grant suits,
How to deny them, who t'advance and who   80
To trash for over-topping, new created
The creatures that were mine, I say, or changed 'em,
Or else new formed 'em; having both the key
Of officer and office, set all hearts i'th'state
To what tune pleased his ear, that now he was   85
The ivy which had hid my princely trunk
And sucked my verdure out on't. Thou attend'st not.

Miranda   O good sir, I do.

Prospero   I pray thee, mark me.
I, thus neglecting worldly ends, all dedicated
To closeness and the bettering of my mind   90
With that, which but by being so retired,
O'er-prized all popular rate, in my false brother
Awaked an evil nature, and my trust,
Like a good parent, did beget of him
A falsehood in its contrary, as great   95
As my trust was, which had indeed no limit,
A confidence sans bound. He being thus lorded,
Not only with what my revenue yielded,
But what my power might else exact, like one
Who having into truth, by telling of it,   100
Made such a sinner of his memory
To credit his own lie, he did believe
He was indeed the duke, out o'th'substitution
And executing the outward face of royalty
With all prerogative. Hence his ambition growing –   105
Dost thou hear?

Miranda   Your tale, sir, would cure deafness.

Prospero   To have no screen between this part he played,
And him he played it for, he needs will be
Absolute Milan. Me, poor man, my library
Was dukedom large enough. Of temporal royalties   110
He thinks me now incapable. Confederates,

Prospero describes how his brother Antonio plotted with the King of Naples to have Prospero and Miranda captured in the middle of the night.

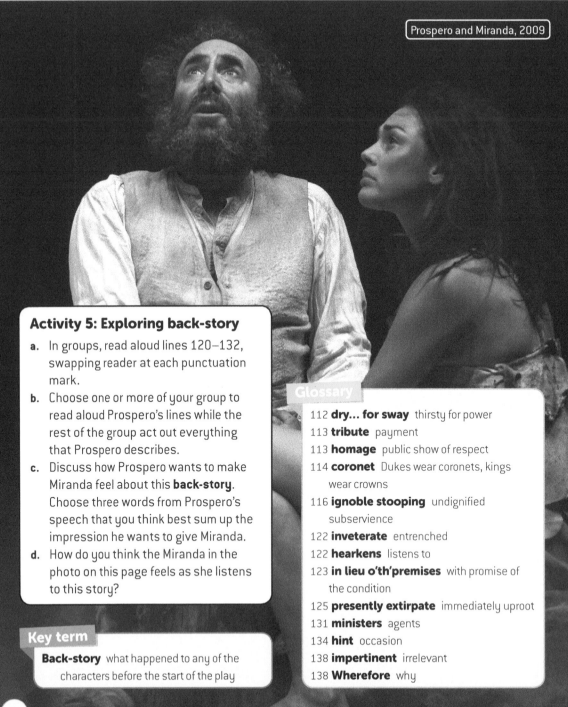

Prospero and Miranda, 2009

Activity 5: Exploring back-story

a. In groups, read aloud lines 120–132, swapping reader at each punctuation mark.

b. Choose one or more of your group to read aloud Prospero's lines while the rest of the group act out everything that Prospero describes.

c. Discuss how Prospero wants to make Miranda feel about this **back-story**. Choose three words from Prospero's speech that you think best sum up the impression he wants to give Miranda.

d. How do you think the Miranda in the photo on this page feels as she listens to this story?

Glossary

112 **dry... for sway** thirsty for power
113 **tribute** payment
113 **homage** public show of respect
114 **coronet** Dukes wear coronets, kings wear crowns
116 **ignoble stooping** undignified subservience
122 **inveterate** entrenched
122 **hearkens** listens to
123 **in lieu o'th'premises** with promise of the condition
125 **presently extirpate** immediately uproot
131 **ministers** agents
134 **hint** occasion
138 **impertinent** irrelevant
138 **Wherefore** why

Key term

Back-story what happened to any of the characters before the start of the play

So dry he was for sway, wi'th'King of Naples
To give him annual tribute, do him homage,
Subject his coronet to his crown, and bend
The dukedom yet unbowed, alas, poor Milan,   115
To most ignoble stooping.

Miranda   O the heavens!

Prospero   Mark his condition and th'event, then tell me
If this might be a brother.

Miranda   I should sin
To think but nobly of my grandmother.
Good wombs have borne bad sons.

Prospero   Now the condition.   120
This King of Naples, being an enemy
To me inveterate, hearkens my brother's suit,
Which was, that he, in lieu o'th'premises
Of homage, and I know not how much tribute,
Should presently extirpate me and mine   125
Out of the dukedom, and confer fair Milan,
With all the honours, on my brother. Whereon,
A treacherous army levied, one midnight
Fated to th'purpose, did Antonio open
The gates of Milan, and i'th'dead of darkness   130
The ministers for th'purpose hurried thence
Me and thy crying self.

Miranda   Alack, for pity.
I, not remembering how I cried out then,
Will cry it o'er again. It is a hint
That wrings mine eyes to't.

Prospero   Hear a little further,   135
And then I'll bring thee to the present business
Which now's upon's, without the which, this story
Were most impertinent.

Miranda   Wherefore did they not
That hour destroy us?

Prospero describes how he and Miranda were taken out to sea and abandoned on a badly equipped boat. They washed up on the island and survived thanks to the supplies given to them by Gonzalo, one of Alonso's men. This included some important books from Prospero's library.

Miranda, 2016

Activity 6: Exploring the theme of hope and fear

a. In pairs, read aloud lines 144–158 with one of you playing Prospero and the other Miranda.

b. Swap roles and read the lines again, this time 'Miranda' repeats out loud any of Prospero's words and phrases that seem connected to fear and hope.

c. Choose one phrase connected to fear and one phrase connected to hope, and create **gestures** for each. For example, you might use your fingers to indicate 'The very rats' as they scuttle along.

d. Speak aloud your two phrases, adding your gestures. Share your ideas with others.

e. Imagine you are Prospero and that you keep a diary. Write two or three diary entries about your time at sea. Describe:
- what you can see, hear, touch, taste and smell
- how you feel about your family
- what you fear and what gives you hope.

Glossary

140 **durst** dared

143 **With colours fairer...** dressed up their actions to look better than they were

144 **bark** small ship

145 **leagues** A league is 3 nautical miles or 5.5 km

146 **butt** barrel

148 **hoist** launched

154 **fortitude** strength

155 **decked** decorated

157 **undergoing stomach** courage to endure

159 **Providence divine** good fortune sent by God

161 **Neapolitan** from Naples

165 **steaded** been useful

Prospero   Well demanded, wench,
          My tale provokes that question. Dear, they durst not,   140
          So dear the love my people bore me; nor set
          A mark so bloody on the business, but
          With colours fairer, painted their foul ends.
          In few, they hurried us aboard a bark,
          Bore us some leagues to sea, where they prepared   145
          A rotten carcass of a butt, not rigged,
          Nor tackle, sail, nor mast. The very rats
          Instinctively have quit it. There they hoist us,
          To cry to the sea that roared to us; to sigh
          To the winds, whose pity sighing back again,   150
          Did us but loving wrong.

Miranda   Alack, what trouble
          Was I then to you?

Prospero   O, a cherubin
          Thou wast that did preserve me. Thou didst smile,
          Infusèd with a fortitude from heaven,
          When I have decked the sea with drops full salt,   155
          Under my burden groaned, which raised in me
          An undergoing stomach, to bear up
          Against what should ensue.

Miranda   How came we ashore?

Prospero By Providence divine.
          Some food we had, and some fresh water, that   160
          A noble Neapolitan, Gonzalo,
          Out of his charity, who being then appointed
          Master of this design, did give us, with
          Rich garments, linens, stuffs and necessaries,
          Which since have steaded much. So, of his gentleness,   165
          Knowing I loved my books, he furnished me
          From mine own library with volumes that
          I prize above my dukedom.

Miranda   Would I might
          But ever see that man.

Miranda asks why Prospero created the storm. He explains that his enemies have come to the island and he must take the opportunity presented by their arrival. He then puts Miranda to sleep and calls for Ariel, his servant, who is a spirit of the island with magical powers.

Miranda, Prospero and Ariel, 2012

Activity 7: Exploring the relationship between Prospero and Ariel

a. In pairs, read aloud lines 187–198 with one of you playing Prospero and the other Ariel.

b. Read the lines again, this time slowly, whispering and emphasising each word.

c. Read the lines again, this time speaking loudly and quickly.

d. Discuss which way of speaking you think best suits Ariel and take your ideas into the next exercise.

e. Swap roles and read the lines again, this time with Ariel standing with his feet rooted to the spot while Prospero moves around him.

f. Keeping the same roles as in task e, read the lines again, this time with Prospero standing still while Ariel moves around.

g. Discuss which way of moving seemed best for showing Ariel's relationship with Prospero.

h. Now create a final performance of these lines, based on the ideas you have explored.

Glossary

174 **vainer** more idle
178 **bountiful Fortune** Fortune was seen as a fickle goddess of luck but here is generous to Prospero
180 **prescience** foresight
181 **zenith** highest point
182 **auspicious star** promising sign of success
183 **court** try to win
183 **omit** ignore
192 **task** instruct
193 **quality** skills; other spirits
196 **beak** prow
197 **waist** middle

Prospero	Now I arise.	
	Sit still, and hear the last of our sea-sorrow.	170

Prospero   Now I arise.
Sit still, and hear the last of our sea-sorrow.   170
Here in this island we arrived, and here
Have I, thy schoolmaster, made thee more profit
Than other princes can that have more time
For vainer hours, and tutors not so careful.

Miranda   Heavens thank you for't. And now, I pray you, sir,   175
For still 'tis beating in my mind, your reason
For raising this sea-storm?

Prospero   Know thus far forth.
By accident most strange, bountiful Fortune,
Now my dear lady, hath mine enemies
Brought to this shore, and by my prescience   180
I find my zenith doth depend upon
A most auspicious star, whose influence
If now I court not, but omit, my fortunes
Will ever after droop. Here cease more questions.
Thou art inclined to sleep. 'Tis a good dullness,   185
And give it way. I know thou canst not choose.

Miranda sleeps

Come away, servant, come. I am ready now.
Approach, my Ariel, come.

Enter Ariel

Ariel   All hail, great master! Grave sir, hail! I come
To answer thy best pleasure, be't to fly,   190
To swim, to dive into the fire, to ride
On the curled clouds. To thy strong bidding, task
Ariel, and all his quality.

Prospero   Hast thou, spirit,
Performed to point the tempest that I bade thee?

Ariel   To every article.   195
I boarded the king's ship, now on the beak,
Now in the waist, the deck, in every cabin,
I flamed amazement. Sometime I'd divide

Ariel continues to describe how he created the storm around the ship, driving everyone on board to distraction until all but the crew jumped into the sea. He assures Prospero that they are all safe and are dispersed around the island, with the king's son on his own.

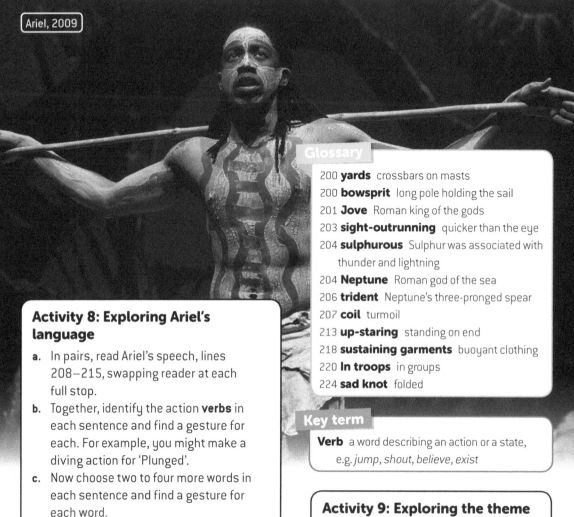

Ariel, 2009

Glossary

200 **yards** crossbars on masts
200 **bowsprit** long pole holding the sail
201 **Jove** Roman king of the gods
203 **sight-outrunning** quicker than the eye
204 **sulphurous** Sulphur was associated with thunder and lightning
204 **Neptune** Roman god of the sea
206 **trident** Neptune's three-pronged spear
207 **coil** turmoil
213 **up-staring** standing on end
218 **sustaining garments** buoyant clothing
220 **In troops** in groups
224 **sad knot** folded

Activity 8: Exploring Ariel's language

a. In pairs, read Ariel's speech, lines 208–215, swapping reader at each full stop.
b. Together, identify the action **verbs** in each sentence and find a gesture for each. For example, you might make a diving action for 'Plunged'.
c. Now choose two to four more words in each sentence and find a gesture for each word.
d. Read the speech aloud together, adding your gestures for the verbs and your chosen words.
e. How do you think the language Ariel uses might indicate how he speaks and moves? For example, do you think he should speak quickly or slowly, move smoothly or jaggedly?

Key term

Verb a word describing an action or a state, e.g. *jump, shout, believe, exist*

Activity 9: Exploring the theme of power and authority

a. Read lines 217–226, swapping reader at each punctuation mark.
b. What powers does Ariel have?
c. What do you learn from this exchange about who has power and who has authority? How would you explain the difference?

And burn in many places, on the topmast,
The yards and bowsprit would I flame distinctly, 200
Then meet and join. Jove's lightning, the precursors
O'th'dreadful thunderclaps, more momentary
And sight-outrunning were not. The fire and cracks
Of sulphurous roaring, the most mighty Neptune
Seem to besiege and make his bold waves tremble, 205
Yea, his dread trident shake.

Prospero   My brave spirit.
Who was so firm, so constant, that this coil
Would not infect his reason?

Ariel   Not a soul
But felt a fever of the mad and played
Some tricks of desperation. All but mariners 210
Plunged in the foaming brine and quit the vessel,
Then all afire with me. The king's son Ferdinand,
With hair up-staring, then like reeds, not hair,
Was the first man that leaped; cried, 'Hell is empty
And all the devils are here.'

Prospero   Why, that's my spirit! 215
But was not this nigh shore?

Ariel   Close by, my master.

Prospero   But are they, Ariel, safe?

Ariel   Not a hair perished.
On their sustaining garments not a blemish,
But fresher than before, and, as thou bad'st me,
In troops I have dispersed them 'bout the isle. 220
The king's son have I landed by himself,
Whom I left cooling of the air with sighs
In an odd angle of the isle, and sitting,
His arms in this sad knot.

Prospero   Of the king's ship,
The Mariners, say how thou hast disposed, 225
And all the rest o'th'fleet?

Ariel describes how he left the crew asleep aboard the ship, harboured in a bay, while the rest of the fleet has sailed on, believing their king to be lost. Prospero plans more work for the day, but Ariel reminds him of his promise to set Ariel free.

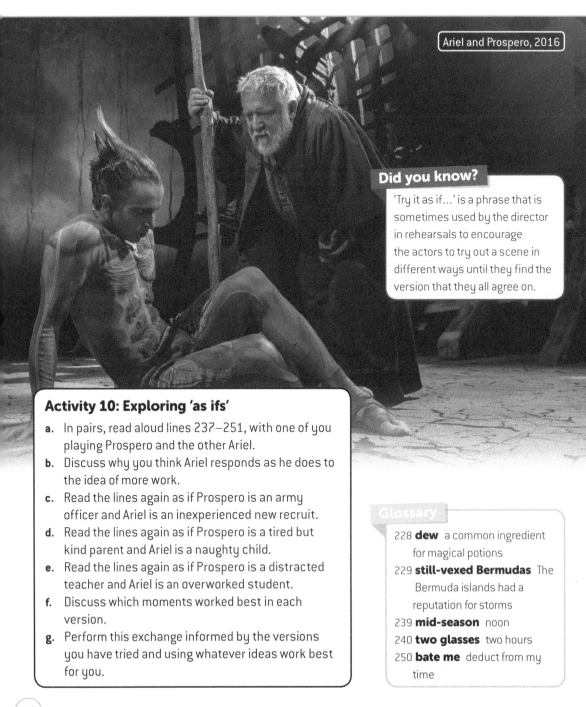

Ariel and Prospero, 2016

Did you know?

'Try it as if...' is a phrase that is sometimes used by the director in rehearsals to encourage the actors to try out a scene in different ways until they find the version that they all agree on.

Activity 10: Exploring 'as ifs'

a. In pairs, read aloud lines 237–251, with one of you playing Prospero and the other Ariel.
b. Discuss why you think Ariel responds as he does to the idea of more work.
c. Read the lines again as if Prospero is an army officer and Ariel is an inexperienced new recruit.
d. Read the lines again as if Prospero is a tired but kind parent and Ariel is a naughty child.
e. Read the lines again as if Prospero is a distracted teacher and Ariel is an overworked student.
f. Discuss which moments worked best in each version.
g. Perform this exchange informed by the versions you have tried and using whatever ideas work best for you.

Glossary

228 **dew** a common ingredient for magical potions
229 **still-vexed Bermudas** The Bermuda islands had a reputation for storms
239 **mid-season** noon
240 **two glasses** two hours
250 **bate me** deduct from my time

Ariel	Safely in harbour
	Is the king's ship, in the deep nook where once
	Thou call'dst me up at midnight to fetch dew
	From the still-vexed Bermudas, there she's hid;
	The mariners all under hatches stowed,

230

Who, with a charm joined to their suffered labour,
I have left asleep. And for the rest o'th'fleet,
Which I dispersed, they all have met again,
And are upon the Mediterranean float
Bound sadly home for Naples,   235
Supposing that they saw the king's ship wrecked
And his great person perish.

Prospero   Ariel, thy charge
Exactly is performed, but there's more work.
What is the time o'th'day?

Ariel   Past the mid-season.

Prospero   At least two glasses. The time 'twixt six and now   240
Must by us both be spent most preciously.

Ariel   Is there more toil? Since thou dost give me pains,
Let me remember thee what thou hast promised,
Which is not yet performed me.

Prospero   How now? Moody?
What is't thou canst demand?

Ariel   My liberty.   245

Prospero   Before the time be out? No more.

Ariel   I prithee,
Remember I have done thee worthy service,
Told thee no lies, made thee no mistakings, served
Without or grudge or grumblings. Thou did promise
To bate me a full year.

Prospero   Dost thou forget   250
From what a torment I did free thee?

Ariel   No.

Prospero reminds Ariel that when he arrived, Ariel had been imprisoned in a tree for 12 years by a witch called Sycorax. Sycorax had died, leaving her son Caliban alone and Ariel still imprisoned. Prospero set Ariel free on condition that Ariel serve him.

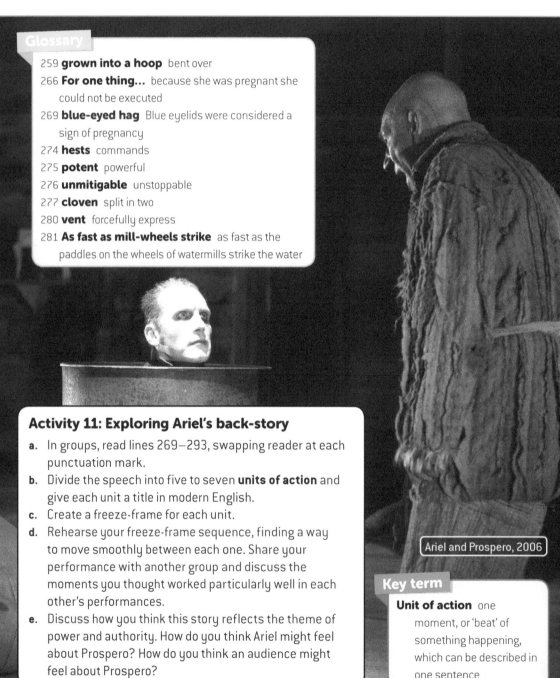

Glossary

259 **grown into a hoop** bent over
266 **For one thing...** because she was pregnant she could not be executed
269 **blue-eyed hag** Blue eyelids were considered a sign of pregnancy
274 **hests** commands
275 **potent** powerful
276 **unmitigable** unstoppable
277 **cloven** split in two
280 **vent** forcefully express
281 **As fast as mill-wheels strike** as fast as the paddles on the wheels of watermills strike the water

Activity 11: Exploring Ariel's back-story

a. In groups, read lines 269–293, swapping reader at each punctuation mark.
b. Divide the speech into five to seven **units of action** and give each unit a title in modern English.
c. Create a freeze-frame for each unit.
d. Rehearse your freeze-frame sequence, finding a way to move smoothly between each one. Share your performance with another group and discuss the moments you thought worked particularly well in each other's performances.
e. Discuss how you think this story reflects the theme of power and authority. How do you think Ariel might feel about Prospero? How do you think an audience might feel about Prospero?

Ariel and Prospero, 2006

Key term

Unit of action one moment, or 'beat' of something happening, which can be described in one sentence

Prospero	Thou dost, and think'st it much to tread the ooze
	Of the salt deep,
	To run upon the sharp wind of the north,
	To do me business in the veins o'th'earth 255
	When it is baked with frost.
Ariel	I do not, sir.
Prospero	Thou liest, malignant thing. Hast thou forgot
	The foul witch Sycorax, who with age and envy
	Was grown into a hoop? Hast thou forgot her?
Ariel	No, sir.
Prospero	Thou hast. Where was she born? Speak, tell me. 260
Ariel	Sir, in Algiers.
Prospero	O, was she so? I must
	Once in a month recount what thou hast been,
	Which thou forget'st. This damned witch Sycorax,
	For mischiefs manifold, and sorceries terrible
	To enter human hearing, from Algiers, 265
	Thou know'st, was banished. For one thing she did
	They would not take her life. Is not this true?
Ariel	Ay, sir.
Prospero	This blue-eyed hag was hither brought with child,
	And here was left by the sailors. Thou, my slave, 270
	As thou report'st thyself, wast then her servant,
	And, for thou wast a spirit too delicate
	To act her earthy and abhorred commands,
	Refusing her grand hests, she did confine thee
	By help of her more potent ministers, 275
	And in her most unmitigable rage,
	Into a cloven pine, within which rift
	Imprisoned thou didst painfully remain
	A dozen years. Within which space she died,
	And left thee there, where thou didst vent thy groans 280
	As fast as mill-wheels strike. Then was this island,

Prospero emphasises the pain Ariel was in whilst trapped and threatens to imprison Ariel in another tree if he complains any more. Ariel apologises. Prospero sends him away to become an invisible sea nymph and then wakes up Miranda.

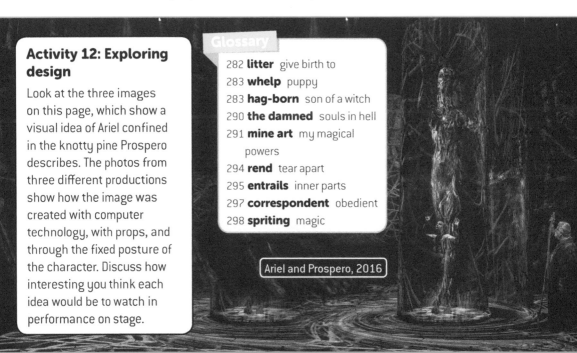

Activity 12: Exploring design

Look at the three images on this page, which show a visual idea of Ariel confined in the knotty pine Prospero describes. The photos from three different productions show how the image was created with computer technology, with props, and through the fixed posture of the character. Discuss how interesting you think each idea would be to watch in performance on stage.

Glossary

282 **litter** give birth to
283 **whelp** puppy
283 **hag-born** son of a witch
290 **the damned** souls in hell
291 **mine art** my magical powers
294 **rend** tear apart
295 **entrails** inner parts
297 **correspondent** obedient
298 **spriting** magic

Ariel and Prospero, 2016

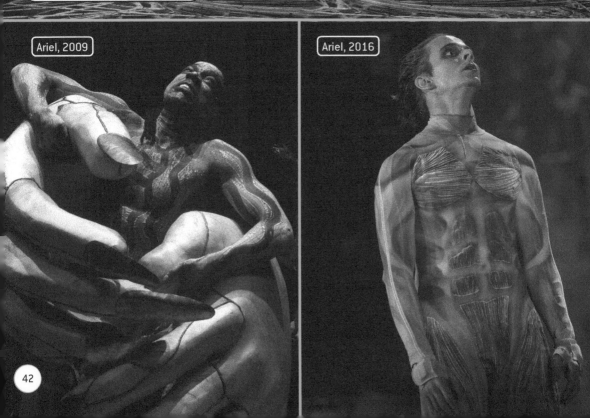

Ariel, 2009

Ariel, 2016

Save for the son that she did litter here,
A freckled whelp, hag-born, not honoured with
A human shape.

Ariel   Yes, Caliban her son.

Prospero   Dull thing, I say so. He, that Caliban   285
Whom now I keep in service. Thou best know'st
What torment I did find thee in. Thy groans
Did make wolves howl and penetrate the breasts
Of ever-angry bears. It was a torment
To lay upon the damned, which Sycorax   290
Could not again undo. It was mine art,
When I arrived and heard thee, that made gape
The pine and let thee out.

Ariel   I thank thee, master.

Prospero   If thou more murmur'st, I will rend an oak
And peg thee in his knotty entrails till   295
Thou hast howled away twelve winters.

Ariel   Pardon, master.
I will be correspondent to command
And do my spriting gently.

Prospero   Do so. And after two days
I will discharge thee.

Ariel   That's my noble master.   300
What shall I do? Say what? What shall I do?

Prospero   Go make thyself like a nymph o'th'sea.
Be subject to no sight but thine and mine, invisible
To every eyeball else. Go take this shape
And hither come in't. Go! Hence, with diligence.   305

Exit Ariel

[To Miranda] Awake, dear heart, awake. Thou hast slept well.
Awake.

Miranda   The strangeness of your story put
Heaviness in me.

Prospero and Miranda visit Caliban. Miranda protests, but Prospero says they need Caliban's services. Prospero calls Caliban with insults and Caliban appears, cursing them both. Prospero responds by promising punishments.

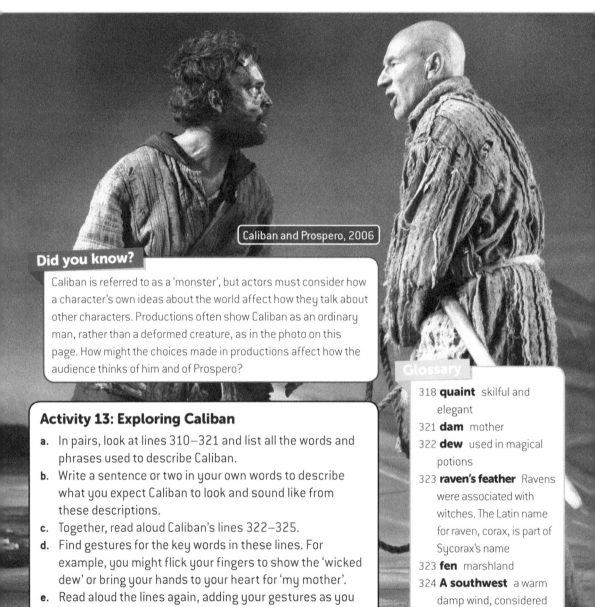

Caliban and Prospero, 2006

Did you know?

Caliban is referred to as a 'monster', but actors must consider how a character's own ideas about the world affect how they talk about other characters. Productions often show Caliban as an ordinary man, rather than a deformed creature, as in the photo on this page. How might the choices made in productions affect how the audience thinks of him and of Prospero?

Activity 13: Exploring Caliban

a. In pairs, look at lines 310–321 and list all the words and phrases used to describe Caliban.
b. Write a sentence or two in your own words to describe what you expect Caliban to look and sound like from these descriptions.
c. Together, read aloud Caliban's lines 322–325.
d. Find gestures for the key words in these lines. For example, you might flick your fingers to show the 'wicked dew' or bring your hands to your heart for 'my mother'.
e. Read aloud the lines again, adding your gestures as you read.
f. How does the way Caliban speaks match Prospero's description of him? In what ways might Caliban's speech surprise an audience?

Glossary

318 **quaint** skilful and elegant
321 **dam** mother
322 **dew** used in magical potions
323 **raven's feather** Ravens were associated with witches. The Latin name for raven, corax, is part of Sycorax's name
323 **fen** marshland
324 **A southwest** a warm damp wind, considered unhealthy
327 **pen** cage
327 **Urchins** goblins in the form of hedgehogs

Prospero	Shake it off. Come on.
	We'll visit Caliban, my slave, who never
	Yields us kind answer.
Miranda	'Tis a villain, sir, 310
	I do not love to look on.
Prospero	But, as 'tis,
	We cannot miss him. He does make our fire,
	Fetch in our wood and serves in offices
	That profit us. What, ho! Slave! Caliban!
	Thou earth, thou! Speak!
Caliban	[Within] There's wood enough within. 315
Prospero	Come forth, I say. There's other business for thee.
	Come, thou tortoise. When?

Enter Ariel like a water-nymph

Fine apparition! My quaint Ariel,
Hark in thine ear.

Prospero whispers to Ariel

Ariel	My lord, it shall be done.

Exit Ariel

Prospero	Thou poisonous slave, got by the devil himself 320
	Upon thy wicked dam, come forth!

Enter Caliban

Caliban	As wicked dew as e'er my mother brushed
	With raven's feather from unwholesome fen
	Drop on you both! A southwest blow on ye
	And blister you all o'er! 325
Prospero	For this, be sure, tonight thou shalt have cramps,
	Side-stitches that shall pen thy breath up. Urchins
	Shall, for that vast of night that they may work,
	All exercise on thee. Thou shalt be pinched
	As thick as honeycomb, each pinch more stinging 330
	Than bees that made 'em.

Caliban claims that Prospero stole the island from him and treats him as a slave. Prospero says his harsh treatment is a punishment for trying to rape Miranda. Although originally Miranda helped Caliban learn to speak, she now thinks he is irredeemably bad.

Caliban, 2009

At the time

Using pages 192–193, find out more about the discoveries in the New World in Shakespeare's time. How does this inform your ideas about Prospero and Caliban's relationship?

Activity 14: Exploring the theme of power and authority

a. In pairs, read aloud Caliban's speech in lines 331–345.

b. Read the lines again. Every time you reach a comma hit your book and every time you reach a full stop or exclamation mark stamp your foot.

c. Face each other and read the speech again. This time whenever you say *me, my* or *mine* tap your chest and whenever you say *thou, thee* or *you* point at your partner.

d. Repeat tasks a–c with Prospero's speech in lines 345–349.

e. Discuss how you think Caliban and Prospero feel about each other.

f. Decide who will play Caliban and who will play Prospero. Then read aloud lines 342–350.

g. Read the lines again, this time as if Caliban did not mean to hurt Miranda but knows Prospero will never believe him.

h. Read the lines again, this time as if Caliban did attack Miranda and says what he means.

i. Read aloud Miranda's speech in lines 351–362, swapping reader at each punctuation mark. Discuss how you think Miranda might feel about Caliban.

Did you know?

In Shakespeare's time, people used 'thou' as a more familiar version of 'you' for people close to them, like friends. 'Thou' was also used to address people of a lower social status. They used 'you' when they wanted to be more polite or formal. 'Thou' was also used when someone was physically closer.

Caliban   I must eat my dinner.
This island's mine by Sycorax my mother,
Which thou tak'st from me. When thou cam'st first,
Thou strok'st me and made much of me, wouldst give me
Water with berries in't, and teach me how   335
To name the bigger light, and how the less,
That burn by day and night, and then I loved thee
And showed thee all the qualities o'th'isle,
The fresh springs, brine-pits, barren place and fertile.
Cursed be I that did so. All the charms   340
Of Sycorax, toads, beetles, bats, light on you!
For I am all the subjects that you have,
Which first was mine own king, and here you sty me
In this hard rock, whiles you do keep from me
The rest o'th'island.

Prospero   Thou most lying slave,   345
Whom stripes may move, not kindness. I have used thee,
Filth as thou art, with humane care, and lodged thee
In mine own cell, till thou didst seek to violate
The honour of my child.

Caliban   O ho, O ho. Would't had been done.
Thou didst prevent me. I had peopled else   350
This isle with Calibans.

Miranda   Abhorrèd slave,
Which any print of goodness wilt not take,
Being capable of all ill. I pitied thee,
Took pains to make thee speak, taught thee each hour
One thing or other. When thou didst not, savage,   355
Know thine own meaning, but wouldst gabble like
A thing most brutish, I endowed thy purposes
With words that made them known. But thy vile race,
Though thou didst learn, had that in't which good natures
Could not abide to be with. Therefore wast thou   360
Deservedly confined into this rock,
Who hadst deserved more than a prison.

Prospero orders Caliban to fetch fuel for the fire. Caliban obeys to avoid the punishments Prospero threatens. Ariel and the other spirits of the island appear, singing and leading Ferdinand. Ariel and the spirits are invisible to everyone on the island except Prospero.

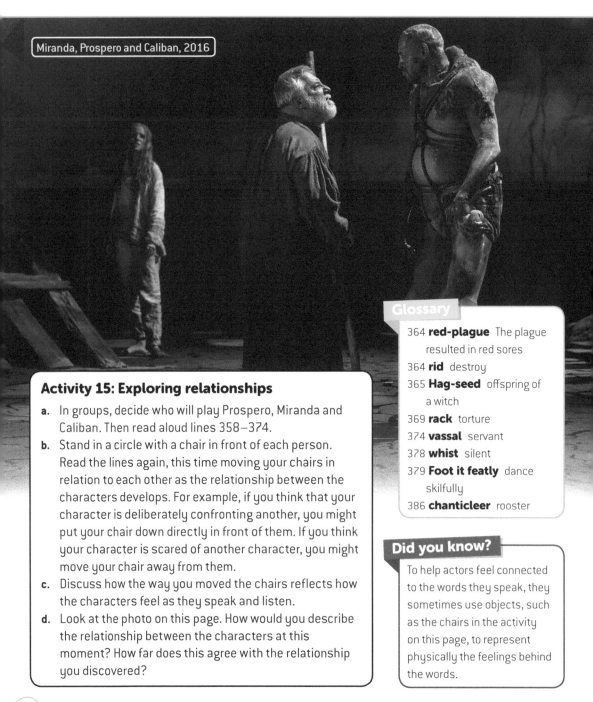

Miranda, Prospero and Caliban, 2016

Activity 15: Exploring relationships

a. In groups, decide who will play Prospero, Miranda and Caliban. Then read aloud lines 358–374.

b. Stand in a circle with a chair in front of each person. Read the lines again, this time moving your chairs in relation to each other as the relationship between the characters develops. For example, if you think that your character is deliberately confronting another, you might put your chair down directly in front of them. If you think your character is scared of another character, you might move your chair away from them.

c. Discuss how the way you moved the chairs reflects how the characters feel as they speak and listen.

d. Look at the photo on this page. How would you describe the relationship between the characters at this moment? How far does this agree with the relationship you discovered?

Glossary

364 **red-plague** The plague resulted in red sores

364 **rid** destroy

365 **Hag-seed** offspring of a witch

369 **rack** torture

374 **vassal** servant

378 **whist** silent

379 **Foot it featly** dance skilfully

386 **chanticleer** rooster

Did you know?

To help actors feel connected to the words they speak, they sometimes use objects, such as the chairs in the activity on this page, to represent physically the feelings behind the words.

Caliban	You taught me language, and my profit on't Is I know how to curse. The red-plague rid you For learning me your language.
Prospero	Hag-seed, hence! Fetch us in fuel, and be quick. Thou'rt best To answer other business. Shrug'st thou, malice? If thou neglect'st or dost unwillingly What I command, I'll rack thee with old cramps, Fill all thy bones with aches, make thee roar, That beasts shall tremble at thy din.
Caliban	No, pray thee. [Aside] I must obey, his art is of such power, It would control my dam's god, Setebos, And make a vassal of him.
Prospero	So, slave, hence!

Exit Caliban. Enter Ferdinand, and Ariel, invisible, playing and singing

Ariel	[Song] Come unto these yellow sands, And then take hands. Curtsied when you have, and kissed The wild waves whist, Foot it featly here and there, And, sweet sprites, bear The burden. Hark, hark.
Spirits	[Within] Bow-wow.
Ariel	The watch-dogs bark.
Spirits	[Within] Bow-wow.
Ariel	Hark, hark. I hear The strain of strutting chanticleer Cry, Cock-a-diddle-dow.
Ferdinand	Where should this music be? I'th'air or th'earth? It sounds no more, and sure it waits upon Some god o'th'island. Sitting on a bank,

365

370

375

380

385

390

Ariel's song describes the death of Ferdinand's father as he drowns in the sea. Prospero points out Ferdinand to Miranda, assuring her that he is not a spirit but a survivor from the shipwreck. She is immediately attracted to him.

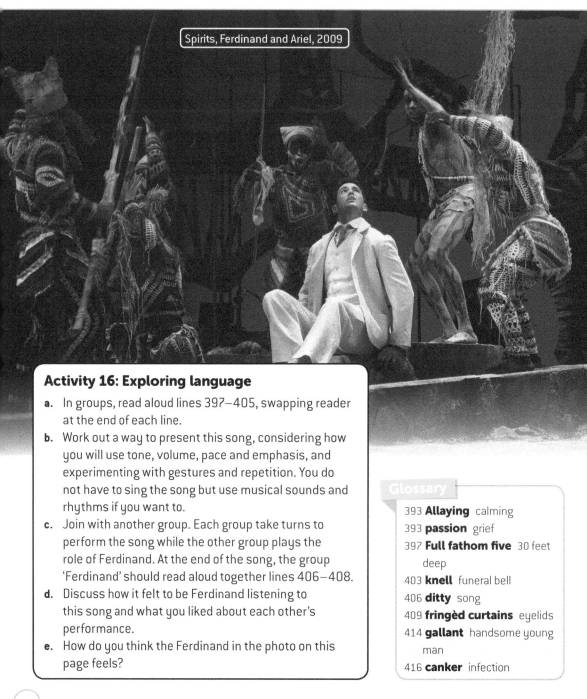

Spirits, Ferdinand and Ariel, 2009

Activity 16: Exploring language

a. In groups, read aloud lines 397–405, swapping reader at the end of each line.

b. Work out a way to present this song, considering how you will use tone, volume, pace and emphasis, and experimenting with gestures and repetition. You do not have to sing the song but use musical sounds and rhythms if you want to.

c. Join with another group. Each group take turns to perform the song while the other group plays the role of Ferdinand. At the end of the song, the group 'Ferdinand' should read aloud together lines 406–408.

d. Discuss how it felt to be Ferdinand listening to this song and what you liked about each other's performance.

e. How do you think the Ferdinand in the photo on this page feels?

Glossary

393 **Allaying** calming
393 **passion** grief
397 **Full fathom five** 30 feet deep
403 **knell** funeral bell
406 **ditty** song
409 **fringèd curtains** eyelids
414 **gallant** handsome young man
416 **canker** infection

Weeping again the king my father's wreck,
This music crept by me upon the waters,
Allaying both their fury and my passion
With its sweet air. Thence I have followed it,
Or it hath drawn me rather, but 'tis gone.   395
No, it begins again.

Ariel   [Song] Full fathom five thy father lies,
Of his bones are coral made;
Those are pearls that were his eyes
Nothing of him that doth fade,   400
But doth suffer a sea-change
Into something rich and strange.
Sea-nymphs hourly ring his knell.

Spirits   [Within] Ding-dong.

Ariel   Hark, now I hear them.

Spirits   [Within] Ding-dong, bell.   405

Ferdinand   The ditty does remember my drowned father.
This is no mortal business, nor no sound
That the earth owes. I hear it now above me.

Prospero   [To Miranda] The fringèd curtains of thine eye advance
And say what thou seest yond.

Miranda   What is't? A spirit?   410
Lord, how it looks about. Believe me, sir,
It carries a brave form. But 'tis a spirit.

Prospero   No, wench, it eats, and sleeps, and hath such senses
As we have, such. This gallant which thou seest
Was in the wreck, and, but he's something stained   415
With grief, that's beauty's canker, thou mightst call him
A goodly person. He hath lost his fellows
And strays about to find 'em.

Miranda   I might call him
A thing divine, for nothing natural
I ever saw so noble.

Ferdinand thinks Miranda is the goddess of the island, but she assures him she is human. He tells Prospero and Miranda that he is the King of Naples, believing his father to be dead. Ferdinand and Miranda have fallen in love at first sight but Prospero pretends to dislike Ferdinand.

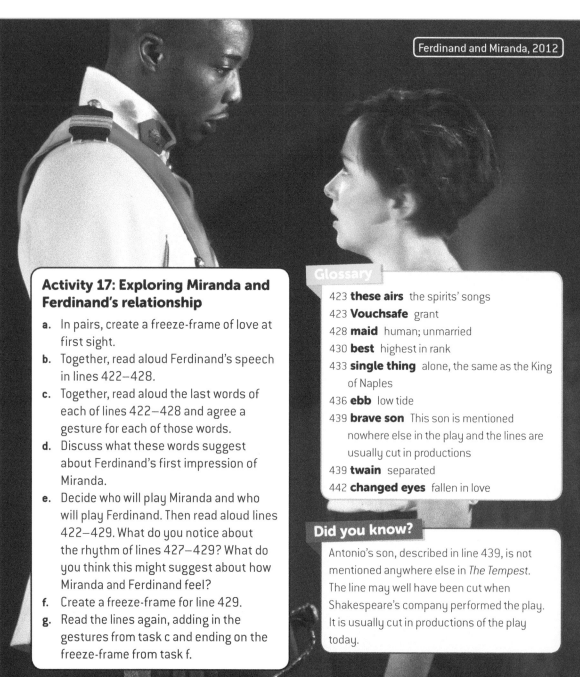

Ferdinand and Miranda, 2012

Activity 17: Exploring Miranda and Ferdinand's relationship

a. In pairs, create a freeze-frame of love at first sight.

b. Together, read aloud Ferdinand's speech in lines 422–428.

c. Together, read aloud the last words of each of lines 422–428 and agree a gesture for each of those words.

d. Discuss what these words suggest about Ferdinand's first impression of Miranda.

e. Decide who will play Miranda and who will play Ferdinand. Then read aloud lines 422–429. What do you notice about the rhythm of lines 427–429? What do you think this might suggest about how Miranda and Ferdinand feel?

f. Create a freeze-frame for line 429.

g. Read the lines again, adding in the gestures from task c and ending on the freeze-frame from task f.

Glossary

423 **these airs** the spirits' songs
423 **Vouchsafe** grant
428 **maid** human; unmarried
430 **best** highest in rank
433 **single thing** alone, the same as the King of Naples
436 **ebb** low tide
439 **brave son** This son is mentioned nowhere else in the play and the lines are usually cut in productions
439 **twain** separated
442 **changed eyes** fallen in love

Did you know?

Antonio's son, described in line 439, is not mentioned anywhere else in The Tempest. The line may well have been cut when Shakespeare's company performed the play. It is usually cut in productions of the play today.

Prospero	[Aside] It goes on, I see,	420
	As my soul prompts it. [To Ariel] Spirit, fine spirit, I'll free thee	
	Within two days for this.	
Ferdinand	Most sure, the goddess	
	On whom these airs attend! Vouchsafe my prayer	
	May know if you remain upon this island,	
	And that you will some good instruction give	425
	How I may bear me here. My prime request,	
	Which I do last pronounce, is, O you wonder,	
	If you be maid or no?	
Miranda	No wonder, sir,	
	But certainly a maid.	
Ferdinand	My language? Heavens!	
	I am the best of them that speak this speech,	430
	Were I but where 'tis spoken.	
Prospero	How? The best?	
	What wert thou if the King of Naples heard thee?	
Ferdinand	A single thing, as I am now, that wonders	
	To hear thee speak of Naples. He does hear me,	
	And that he does, I weep. Myself am Naples,	435
	Who with mine eyes, never since at ebb, beheld	
	The king my father wrecked.	
Miranda	Alack, for mercy!	
Ferdinand	Yes, faith, and all his lords, the Duke of Milan	
	And his brave son being twain.	
Prospero	[Aside] The Duke of Milan	
	And his more braver daughter could control thee	440
	If now 'twere fit to do't. At the first sight	
	They have changed eyes. Delicate Ariel,	
	I'll set thee free for this. [To Ferdinand] A word, good sir,	
	I fear you have done yourself some wrong, a word.	
Miranda	[Aside] Why speaks my father so ungently? This	445
	Is the third man that e'er I saw, the first	

Prospero tells the audience he intends to test Ferdinand's love for Miranda and then accuses Ferdinand of spying. Miranda tries to argue for him and Ferdinand draws his sword to defend himself. Prospero puts a spell on Ferdinand to stop him moving.

Ferdinand, 2016

Activity 18: Exploring the magic of theatre

a. In groups, decide who will play Prospero, Miranda, Ferdinand, Ariel and the other spirits. Then read aloud lines 453–474.

b. Read the lines again, but as you speak and listen, keep choosing between the following movements:
- Take a step towards another character.
- Take a step away from another character.
- Turn towards another character.
- Turn away from another character.
- Stand still.

Try to make instinctive choices rather than planning what to do.

c. Discuss which movement choices worked well to make the action of the lines and the feelings of the characters clear for an audience, and which you want to change.

d. Noting the stage direction after line 467, decide how you want to show the magic of Ferdinand becoming charmed. Perhaps the spirits are involved?

e. Reflecting on this discussion, repeat task b, aiming to make the meaning of your lines clear for the audience and showing clearly that Ferdinand is charmed.

Glossary
450 **Soft** wait a moment
452 **uneasy** difficult
464 **fresh-brook mussels** inedible shellfish
466 **entertainment** treatment
470 **My foot my tutor?** Should an inferior part of me tell me what to do?

Did you know?
The term 'the magic of theatre' is often used to explain how in a theatre production the audience is encouraged to use its imagination, along with the actors, in order to create events that might otherwise seem unrealistic.

That e'er I sighed for. Pity move my father
To be inclined my way.

Ferdinand   O, if a virgin,
And your affection not gone forth, I'll make you
The Queen of Naples.

Prospero   Soft, sir, one word more.   450
[Aside] They are both in either's powers, but this swift business
I must uneasy make, lest too light winning
Make the prize light. [To Ferdinand] One word more. I charge thee
That thou attend me. Thou dost here usurp
The name thou ow'st not, and hast put thyself   455
Upon this island as a spy, to win it
From me, the lord on't.

Ferdinand   No, as I am a man.

Miranda There's nothing ill can dwell in such a temple.
If the ill-spirit have so fair a house,
Good things will strive to dwell with't.

Prospero   Follow me.   460
Speak not you for him, he's a traitor. Come,
I'll manacle thy neck and feet together.
Seawater shalt thou drink. Thy food shall be
The fresh-brook mussels, withered roots and husks
Wherein the acorn cradled. Follow.

Ferdinand   No!   465
I will resist such entertainment till
Mine enemy has more power.

He draws, and is charmed from moving

Miranda   O dear father,
Make not too rash a trial of him, for
He's gentle, and not fearful.

Prospero   What, I say,
My foot my tutor? [To Ferdinand] Put thy sword up, traitor,   470
Who mak'st a show but dar'st not strike, thy conscience

Prospero tells Miranda to stop defending Ferdinand and that there are far better men in the world. Ferdinand submits to Prospero's powers with the hope that he will be able to see Miranda each day.

Miranda, Prospero and Ferdinand, 2006

472 **ward** position of defence
474 **Beseech** beg
475 **Hence** away
476 **surety** guarantor
477 **chide** punish
485 **nerves** sinews
486 **vigour** strength
487 **spirits** senses

Activity 19: Exploring asides

a. In groups, read Prospero's lines 494–496, which include an **aside**, swapping reader at each full stop.
b. Sometimes a play script can be confusing to read because it is meant to be performed. The following performance tasks explore who Prospero is addressing. Decide who will play Prospero, Miranda, Ferdinand and Ariel.
c. Create a freeze-frame, beginning with Prospero. Then add in the other characters, deciding whether they are close to Prospero or further away, facing him or facing away. How close together are Ferdinand and Miranda?
d. Now bring the freeze-frame to life with Prospero speaking aloud lines 494–496 and addressing each sentence to whomever he thinks he should, remembering that addressing the audience is an option.

Key term

Aside when a character addresses a remark to the audience, or to another character, that other characters on the stage do not hear

	Is so possessed with guilt. Come from thy ward,	
	For I can here disarm thee with this stick,	
	And make thy weapon drop.	

Miranda   Beseech you, father.

Prospero   Hence! Hang not on my garments.

Miranda   Sir, have pity.   475
                 I'll be his surety.

Prospero   Silence! One word more
                 Shall make me chide thee, if not hate thee. What,
                 An advocate for an imposter? Hush.
                 Thou think'st there is no more such shapes as he,
                 Having seen but him and Caliban. Foolish wench,   480
                 To th'most of men this is a Caliban,
                 And they to him are angels.

Miranda   My affections
                 Are then most humble. I have no ambition
                 To see a goodlier man.

Prospero   [To Ferdinand] Come on, obey.
                 Thy nerves are in their infancy again   485
                 And have no vigour in them.

Ferdinand   So they are.
                 My spirits, as in a dream, are all bound up.
                 My father's loss, the weakness which I feel,
                 The wreck of all my friends, nor this man's threats,
                 To whom I am subdued, are but light to me,   490
                 Might I but through my prison once a day
                 Behold this maid. All corners else o'th'earth
                 Let liberty make use of; space enough
                 Have I in such a prison.

Prospero   [Aside] It works. [To Ferdinand] Come on.
                 Thou hast done well, fine Ariel! Follow me.   495
                 Hark what thou else shalt do me.

Miranda   [To Ferdinand] Be of comfort.

Miranda tells Ferdinand that her father does not normally behave like this. Prospero promises Ariel he shall soon be free provided he carries out all of Prospero's commands.

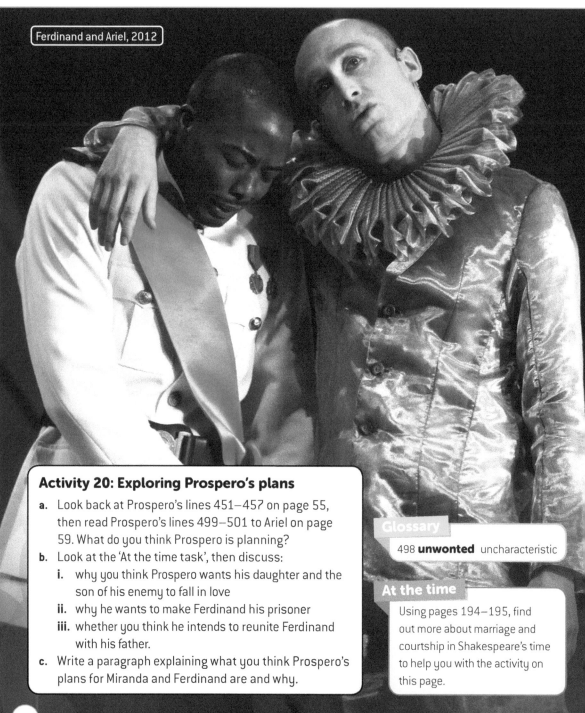

Ferdinand and Ariel, 2012

Activity 20: Exploring Prospero's plans

a. Look back at Prospero's lines 451–457 on page 55, then read Prospero's lines 499–501 to Ariel on page 59. What do you think Prospero is planning?

b. Look at the 'At the time task', then discuss:
   i. why you think Prospero wants his daughter and the son of his enemy to fall in love
   ii. why he wants to make Ferdinand his prisoner
   iii. whether you think he intends to reunite Ferdinand with his father.

c. Write a paragraph explaining what you think Prospero's plans for Miranda and Ferdinand are and why.

Glossary

498 **unwonted** uncharacteristic

At the time

Using pages 194–195, find out more about marriage and courtship in Shakespeare's time to help you with the activity on this page.

My father's of a better nature, sir,
Than he appears by speech. This is unwonted
Which now came from him.

Prospero   [To Ariel] Thou shalt be as free
As mountain winds; but then exactly do   500
All points of my command.

Ariel   To th'syllable.

Prospero   [To Ferdinand] Come, follow. [To Miranda] Speak not for him.

Exeunt

Exploring Act 1

Miranda, 2016

Activity 1: Exploring the theme of power and authority in Act 1

a. Discuss how Shakespeare develops the theme of power and authority in Act 1 by comparing:
    - what power each of the characters we meet has to affect the lives of others
    - what authority each of them has to control the lives of others.

b. Write a brief essay (no more than 400 words) to answer the question: 'How does Shakespeare present the theme of power and authority in Act 1 of *The Tempest*?' You could include:
    - the ideas you discussed in task a, including examples from the text of what characters say and do
    - what you have noticed about how the **plot** is structured in Act 1
    - how Shakespeare encourages the audience to think about what could happen next.

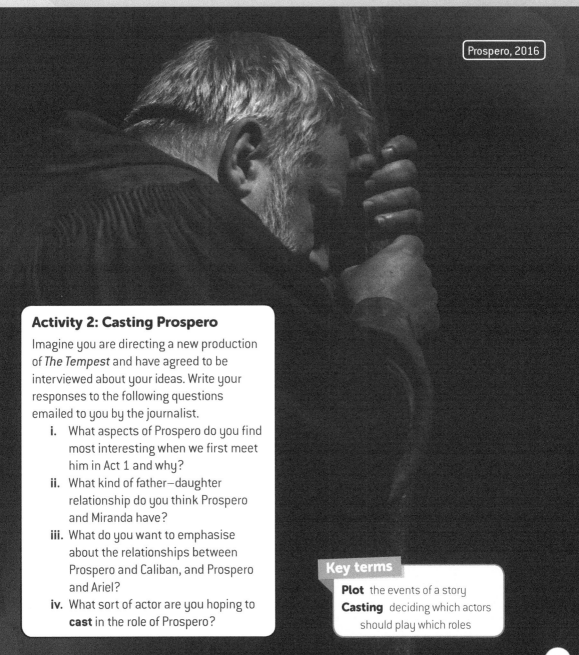

Prospero, 2016

Activity 2: Casting Prospero

Imagine you are directing a new production of *The Tempest* and have agreed to be interviewed about your ideas. Write your responses to the following questions emailed to you by the journalist.

   i. What aspects of Prospero do you find most interesting when we first meet him in Act 1 and why?

  ii. What kind of father–daughter relationship do you think Prospero and Miranda have?

 iii. What do you want to emphasise about the relationships between Prospero and Caliban, and Prospero and Ariel?

 iv. What sort of actor are you hoping to **cast** in the role of Prospero?

Key terms

Plot the events of a story
Casting deciding which actors should play which roles

Gonzalo tries to comfort Alonso by pointing out how lucky they are to have survived the shipwreck. Sebastian and Antonio make fun of Gonzalo.

Gonzalo, Antonio and Sebastian, 2016

Activity 1: Exploring staging

Playscripts can sometimes be confusing to read because they are written to be performed.

a. In groups, decide who will play Gonzalo, Alonso, Sebastian and Antonio. Add Adrian and Francisco depending on the size of your group.

b. Read aloud lines 6–21, remaining seated.

c. Read the lines again on your feet, working out how close you think the characters are to each other and who is talking to whom. Consider whether Gonzalo can hear what Sebastian and Antonio are saying, what Alonso is doing while the other characters speak, and what Adrian and Francisco are doing.

d. Look at the photo on this page and discuss which moment you think is being shown.

Glossary

3 **hint** occasion

11 **The visitor will not give him o'er so** Gonzalo is like a religious adviser who won't give up

14 **Tell** count, as in counting that 'the watch of his wit' has struck one

16 **dollar** a silver coin

17 **Dolour** sorrow

21 **spendthrift** someone who spends money irresponsibly

Key term

Staging the process of selecting, adapting and developing the stage space in which a play will be performed

Act 2 | Scene 1

Enter Alonso, Sebastian, Antonio, Gonzalo, Adrian, Francisco and others

Gonzalo	[To Alonso] Beseech you, sir, be merry. You have cause,
	So have we all, of joy, for our escape
	Is much beyond our loss. Our hint of woe
	Is common. Every day some sailor's wife,
	The masters of some merchant, and the merchant
	Have just our theme of woe. But for the miracle,
	I mean our preservation, few in millions
	Can speak like us. Then wisely, good sir, weigh
	Our sorrow with our comfort.

5

Alonso   Prithee, peace.

Sebastian   [Aside to Antonio] He receives comfort like cold porridge.   10

Antonio   The visitor will not give him o'er so.

Sebastian   Look, he's winding up the watch of his wit. By and by it will
strike.

Gonzalo   Sir—

Sebastian   One. Tell.

Gonzalo   When every grief is entertained
That's offered, comes to th'entertainer—   15

Sebastian   A dollar.

Gonzalo   Dolour comes to him, indeed. You have spoken truer than you
purposed.

Sebastian   You have taken it wiselier than I meant you should.

Gonzalo   Therefore, my lord—   20

Antonio   Fie, what a spendthrift is he of his tongue.

Adrian joins Gonzalo in trying to comfort Alonso by describing the island positively. Sebastian and Antonio continue to make snide remarks.

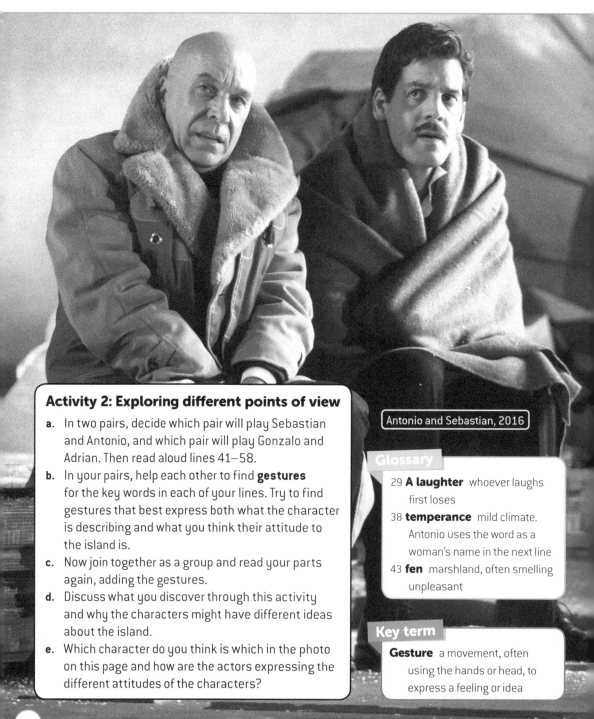

Antonio and Sebastian, 2016

Activity 2: Exploring different points of view

a. In two pairs, decide which pair will play Sebastian and Antonio, and which pair will play Gonzalo and Adrian. Then read aloud lines 41–58.

b. In your pairs, help each other to find **gestures** for the key words in each of your lines. Try to find gestures that best express both what the character is describing and what you think their attitude to the island is.

c. Now join together as a group and read your parts again, adding the gestures.

d. Discuss what you discover through this activity and why the characters might have different ideas about the island.

e. Which character do you think is which in the photo on this page and how are the actors expressing the different attitudes of the characters?

Glossary

29 **A laughter** whoever laughs first loses

38 **temperance** mild climate. Antonio uses the word as a woman's name in the next line

43 **fen** marshland, often smelling unpleasant

Key term

Gesture a movement, often using the hands or head, to express a feeling or idea

Alonso	I prithee, spare.
Gonzalo	Well, I have done. But yet—
Sebastian	He will be talking.
Antonio	Which, of he or Adrian, for a good wager, first begins to crow?
Sebastian	The old cock.
Antonio	The cockerel.
Sebastian	Done. The wager?
Antonio	A laughter.
Sebastian	A match.
Adrian	Though this island seem to be desert—
Sebastian	Ha, ha, ha!
Antonio	So, you're paid.
Adrian	Uninhabitable and almost inaccessible—
Sebastian	Yet—
Adrian	Yet—
Antonio	He could not miss't.
Adrian	It must needs be of subtle, tender and delicate temperance.
Antonio	Temperance was a delicate wench.
Sebastian	Ay, and a subtle, as he most learnedly delivered.
Adrian	The air breathes upon us here most sweetly.
Sebastian	As if it had lungs, and rotten ones.
Antonio	Or as 'twere perfumed by a fen.
Gonzalo	Here is everything advantageous to life.
Antonio	True, save means to live.
Sebastian	Of that there's none, or little.

25

30

35

40

45

Gonzalo continues to be positive, commenting on how their clothes are undamaged from being soaked in the sea. We learn that the nobles had been sailing back to Naples after the wedding of Alonso's daughter Claribel to the King of Tunis in Africa.

Activity 3: Exploring design

a. In pairs, read aloud Gonzalo's lines 59–61.
b. Look at the photos on this page of Alonso from three different productions. Discuss what each costume suggests about Alonso and about the world of the play the designer wanted to create. Which design do you prefer and why?

Did you know?

Costume designers produce detailed drawings of what each character will wear. They read the script and pick up all the clues that are in it about the characters and the situations they are in. Then they consider other elements of the design of the production, such as time period and setting.

Alonso, 2006

Alonso, 2012

Alonso, 2009

Glossary

49 **eye of** hint of
58 **pocket up** conceal
64 **widow Dido** The story of Dido and Aeneas was well known in Shakespeare's time. Dido was queen of Carthage, close to Tunis. She and Aeneas fell in love but he left her. She then committed suicide
73 **miraculous harp** a reference to the Greek story of Amphion, whose music rebuilt the walls of Thebes

Gonzalo	How lush and lusty the grass looks! How green!
Antonio	The ground indeed is tawny.
Sebastian	With an eye of green in't.
Antonio	He misses not much. 50
Sebastian	No, he doth but mistake the truth totally.
Gonzalo	But the rarity of it is, which is indeed almost beyond credit—
Sebastian	As many vouched rarities are.
Gonzalo	That our garments, being, as they were, drenched in the sea, hold notwithstanding their freshness and glosses, being rather new-dyed 55 than stained with salt water.
Antonio	If but one of his pockets could speak, would it not say he lies?
Sebastian	Ay, or very falsely pocket up his report.
Gonzalo	Methinks our garments are now as fresh as when we put them on first in Afric, at the marriage of the king's fair daughter Claribel 60 to the King of Tunis.
Sebastian	'Twas a sweet marriage, and we prosper well in our return.
Adrian	Tunis was never graced before with such a paragon to their queen.
Gonzalo	Not since widow Dido's time.
Antonio	Widow? A pox o'that! How came that 'widow' in? Widow Dido! 65
Sebastian	What if he had said 'widower Aeneas' too? Good lord, how you take it!
Adrian	'Widow Dido', said you? You make me study of that. She was of Carthage, not of Tunis.
Gonzalo	This Tunis, sir, was Carthage. 70
Adrian	Carthage?
Gonzalo	I assure you, Carthage.
Antonio	His word is more than the miraculous harp.

Sebastian and Antonio continue to make fun of Gonzalo. Alonso responds to Gonzalo by saying he regrets the marriage of his daughter because he has now lost both her and his son. Francisco says he saw Ferdinand swimming to shore.

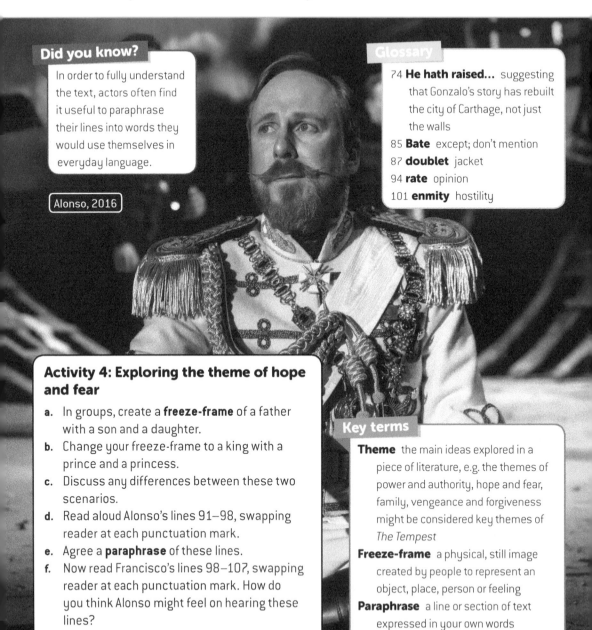

Did you know?

In order to fully understand the text, actors often find it useful to paraphrase their lines into words they would use themselves in everyday language.

Alonso, 2016

Glossary

74 **He hath raised...** suggesting that Gonzalo's story has rebuilt the city of Carthage, not just the walls

85 **Bate** except; don't mention

87 **doublet** jacket

94 **rate** opinion

101 **enmity** hostility

Activity 4: Exploring the theme of hope and fear

a. In groups, create a **freeze-frame** of a father with a son and a daughter.

b. Change your freeze-frame to a king with a prince and a princess.

c. Discuss any differences between these two scenarios.

d. Read aloud Alonso's lines 91–98, swapping reader at each punctuation mark.

e. Agree a **paraphrase** of these lines.

f. Now read Francisco's lines 98–107, swapping reader at each punctuation mark. How do you think Alonso might feel on hearing these lines?

g. The audience knows that Ferdinand is alive. How do you think this **dramatic irony** might affect how they watch this scene?

Key terms

Theme the main ideas explored in a piece of literature, e.g. the themes of power and authority, hope and fear, family, vengeance and forgiveness might be considered key themes of *The Tempest*

Freeze-frame a physical, still image created by people to represent an object, place, person or feeling

Paraphrase a line or section of text expressed in your own words

Dramatic irony when the audience knows something that some characters in the play do not

Sebastian	He hath raised the wall and houses too.
Antonio	What impossible matter will he make easy next?
Sebastian	I think he will carry this island home in his pocket and give it his son for an apple.
Antonio	And, sowing the kernels of it in the sea, bring forth more islands.
Gonzalo	Ay.
Antonio	Why, in good time.
Gonzalo	[To Alonso] Sir, we were talking that our garments seem now as fresh as when we were at Tunis at the marriage of your daughter, who is now queen.
Antonio	And the rarest that e'er came there.
Sebastian	Bate, I beseech you, widow Dido.
Antonio	O, widow Dido? Ay, widow Dido.
Gonzalo	Is not, sir, my doublet as fresh as the first day I wore it? I mean, in a sort—
Antonio	That sort was well fished for.
Gonzalo	When I wore it at your daughter's marriage.
Alonso	You cram these words into mine ears against The stomach of my sense. Would I had never Married my daughter there. For, coming thence, My son is lost and, in my rate, she too, Who is so far from Italy removed I ne'er again shall see her. O thou mine heir Of Naples and of Milan, what strange fish Hath made his meal on thee?
Francisco	Sir, he may live. I saw him beat the surges under him, And ride upon their backs. He trod the water, Whose enmity he flung aside, and breasted The surge most swollen that met him. His bold head

75

80

85

90

95

100

69

Sebastian criticises Alonso for agreeing to the marriage of Claribel to an African king against the advice of others and the wishes of Claribel herself. He says Alonso only has himself to blame for what has happened.

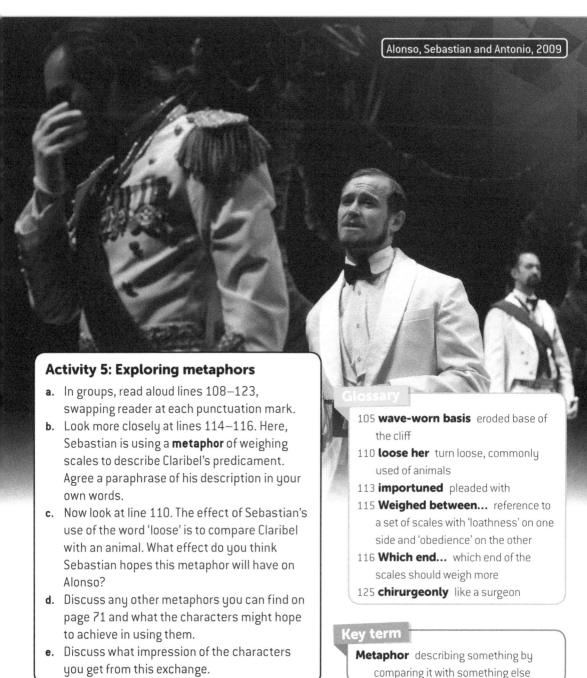

Alonso, Sebastian and Antonio, 2009

Activity 5: Exploring metaphors

a. In groups, read aloud lines 108–123, swapping reader at each punctuation mark.

b. Look more closely at lines 114–116. Here, Sebastian is using a **metaphor** of weighing scales to describe Claribel's predicament. Agree a paraphrase of his description in your own words.

c. Now look at line 110. The effect of Sebastian's use of the word 'loose' is to compare Claribel with an animal. What effect do you think Sebastian hopes this metaphor will have on Alonso?

d. Discuss any other metaphors you can find on page 71 and what the characters might hope to achieve in using them.

e. Discuss what impression of the characters you get from this exchange.

Glossary

105 **wave-worn basis** eroded base of the cliff

110 **loose her** turn loose, commonly used of animals

113 **importuned** pleaded with

115 **Weighed between...** reference to a set of scales with 'loathness' on one side and 'obedience' on the other

116 **Which end...** which end of the scales should weigh more

125 **chirurgeonly** like a surgeon

Key term

Metaphor describing something by comparing it with something else

'Bove the contentious waves he kept, and oared
Himself with his good arms in lusty stroke
To the shore, that o'er his wave-worn basis bowed,   105
As stooping to relieve him. I not doubt
He came alive to land.

Alonso   No, no, he's gone.

Sebastian   Sir, you may thank yourself for this great loss,
That would not bless our Europe with your daughter,
But rather loose her to an African,   110
Where she, at least, is banished from your eye,
Who hath cause to wet the grief on't.

Alonso   Prithee, peace.

Sebastian   You were kneeled to and importuned otherwise
By all of us; and the fair soul herself
Weighed between loathness and obedience at   115
Which end o'the beam should bow. We have lost your son,
I fear, forever. Milan and Naples have
More widows in them of this business' making
Than we bring men to comfort them. The fault's your own.

Alonso   So is the dearest o'th'loss.

Gonzalo   My lord Sebastian,   120
The truth you speak doth lack some gentleness,
And time to speak it in. You rub the sore,
When you should bring the plaster.

Sebastian   Very well.

Antonio   And most chirurgeonly.   125

Gonzalo   [To Alonso] It is foul weather in us all, good sir,
When you are cloudy.

Sebastian   Foul weather?

Antonio   Very foul.

Gonzalo offers a positive vision of how he would rule the island.

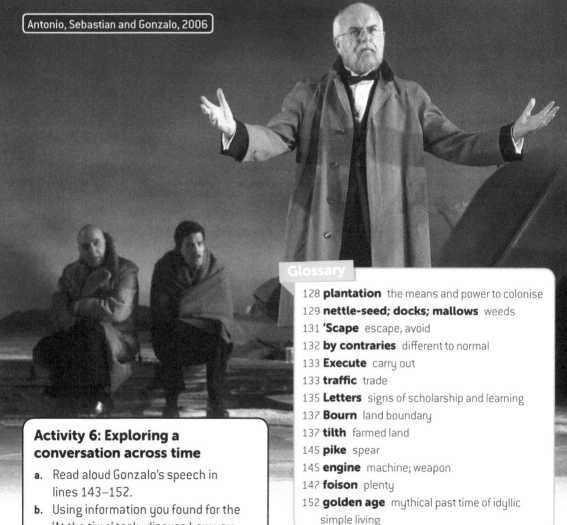

Antonio, Sebastian and Gonzalo, 2006

Activity 6: Exploring a conversation across time

a. Read aloud Gonzalo's speech in lines 143–152.

b. Using information you found for the 'At the time' task, discuss how you think Gonzalo's lines reflect ideas in Shakespeare's time about the New World.

c. Look at the photo on this page from a production where the director chose to set the island in the Arctic. How do you think this very particular setting might affect the way the audience understands Gonzalo's lines?

At the time

In Shakespeare's time, exploration and trade were opening up the new world of the Americas and the stories that came back to the old world of Europe were affecting people's ideas of government. Using pages 192–193, find out more about Jacobean ideas of Commonwealth and the New World.

Gonzalo	[To Alonso] Had I plantation of this isle, my lord—
Antonio	He'd sow't with nettle-seed.
Sebastian	Or docks, or mallows.
Gonzalo	And were the king on't, what would I do?

130

Sebastian	'Scape being drunk for want of wine.

Gonzalo	I'th'commonwealth I would by contraries
	Execute all things. For no kind of traffic
	Would I admit, no name of magistrate.
	Letters should not be known. Riches, poverty,
	And use of service, none. Contract, succession,
	Bourn, bound of land, tilth, vineyard, none.
	No use of metal, corn, or wine, or oil.
	No occupation, all men idle, all.
	And women too, but innocent and pure.
	No sovereignty—

135

140

Sebastian	Yet he would be king on't.
Antonio	The latter end of his commonwealth forgets the beginning.

Gonzalo	All things in common nature should produce
	Without sweat or endeavour. Treason, felony,
	Sword, pike, knife, gun, or need of any engine
	Would I not have; but nature should bring forth,
	Of it own kind, all foison, all abundance,
	To feed my innocent people.

145

Sebastian	No marrying 'mong his subjects?
Antonio	None, man, all idle – whores and knaves.

150

Gonzalo	I would with such perfection govern, sir,
	T'excel the golden age.
Sebastian	'Save his majesty!
Antonio	Long live Gonzalo!
Gonzalo	And, do you mark me, sir?

Gonzalo spars verbally with Sebastian and Antonio. Ariel enters, invisible to the nobles, and puts Gonzalo, Adrian and Francisco to sleep. Alonso comments on how quickly they fell asleep and then falls asleep himself.

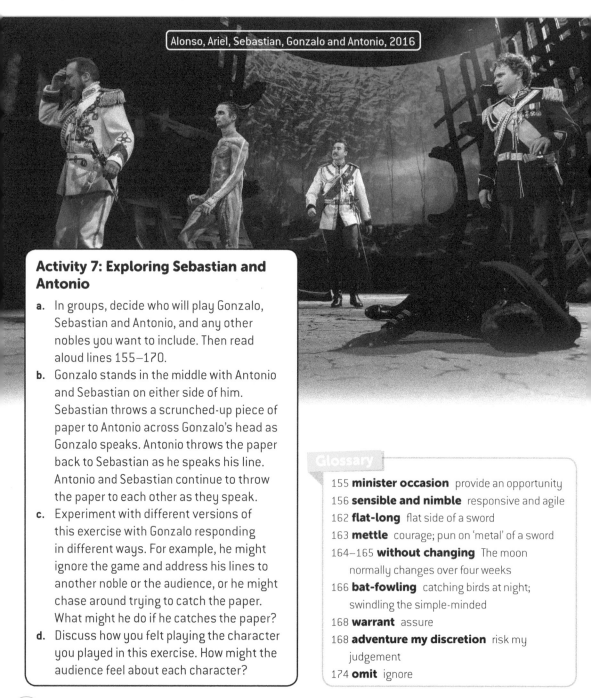

Alonso, Ariel, Sebastian, Gonzalo and Antonio, 2016

Activity 7: Exploring Sebastian and Antonio

a. In groups, decide who will play Gonzalo, Sebastian and Antonio, and any other nobles you want to include. Then read aloud lines 155–170.

b. Gonzalo stands in the middle with Antonio and Sebastian on either side of him. Sebastian throws a scrunched-up piece of paper to Antonio across Gonzalo's head as Gonzalo speaks. Antonio throws the paper back to Sebastian as he speaks his line. Antonio and Sebastian continue to throw the paper to each other as they speak.

c. Experiment with different versions of this exercise with Gonzalo responding in different ways. For example, he might ignore the game and address his lines to another noble or the audience, or he might chase around trying to catch the paper. What might he do if he catches the paper?

d. Discuss how you felt playing the character you played in this exercise. How might the audience feel about each character?

Glossary

155 **minister occasion** provide an opportunity
156 **sensible and nimble** responsive and agile
162 **flat-long** flat side of a sword
163 **mettle** courage; pun on 'metal' of a sword
164–165 **without changing** The moon normally changes over four weeks
166 **bat-fowling** catching birds at night; swindling the simple-minded
168 **warrant** assure
168 **adventure my discretion** risk my judgement
174 **omit** ignore

Alonso	Prithee, no more. Thou dost talk nothing to me.
Gonzalo	I do well believe your highness, and did it to minister occasion to 155 these gentlemen, who are of such sensible and nimble lungs that they always use to laugh at nothing.
Antonio	'Twas you we laughed at.
Gonzalo	Who in this kind of merry fooling am nothing to you; so you may continue and laugh at nothing still. 160
Antonio	What a blow was there given.
Sebastian	An it had not fallen flat-long.
Gonzalo	You are gentlemen of brave mettle. You would lift the moon out of her sphere, if she would continue in it five weeks without changing. 165

Enter Ariel, invisible, playing solemn music

Sebastian	We would so, and then go a bat-fowling.
Antonio	Nay, good my lord, be not angry.
Gonzalo	No, I warrant you. I will not adventure my discretion so weakly. Will you laugh me asleep, for I am very heavy?
Antonio	Go sleep, and hear us. 170

All sleep except Alonso, Sebastian and Antonio

Alonso	What, all so soon asleep? I wish mine eyes Would, with themselves, shut up my thoughts. I find They are inclined to do so.
Sebastian	Please you, sir, Do not omit the heavy offer of it. It seldom visits sorrow. When it doth, 175 It is a comforter.
Antonio	We two, my lord, Will guard your person while you take your rest, And watch your safety.
Alonso	Thank you. Wondrous heavy.

Sebastian and Antonio are amazed at how the other nobles have fallen asleep while they are both left wide awake. Antonio begins to suggest how Sebastian could take advantage of this situation to become king himself.

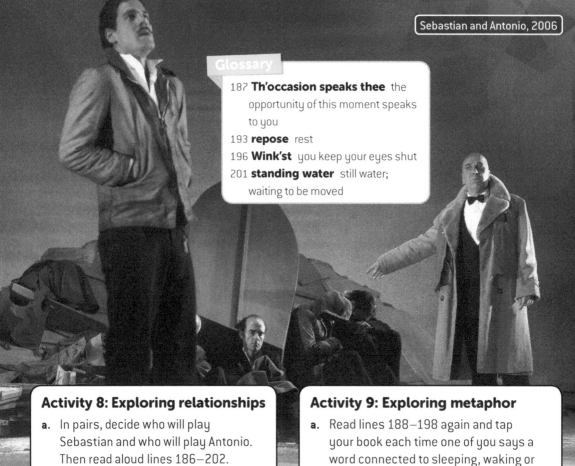

Sebastian and Antonio, 2006

Glossary

187 **Th'occasion speaks thee** the opportunity of this moment speaks to you

193 **repose** rest

196 **Wink'st** you keep your eyes shut

201 **standing water** still water; waiting to be moved

Activity 8: Exploring relationships

a. In pairs, decide who will play Sebastian and who will play Antonio. Then read aloud lines 186–202.

b. Read the lines again, this time with Sebastian rooted to the spot while Antonio moves around anywhere he pleases.

c. Read the lines again with Antonio rooted to the spot while Sebastian moves around as he pleases.

d. Discuss which version worked better and why. What do you think Antonio is trying to get Sebastian to do in this exchange?

Activity 9: Exploring metaphor

a. Read lines 188–198 again and tap your book each time one of you says a word connected to sleeping, waking or speaking.

b. Why do you think Sebastian and Antonio use this **extended metaphor** of being in a dream? Write a paragraph explaining this metaphor and why it is effective.

Key term

Extended metaphor describing something by comparing it to something else over several lines

Alonso sleeps. Exit Ariel

Sebastian	What a strange drowsiness possesses them.
Antonio	It is the quality o'th'climate.
Sebastian	Why 180 Doth it not then our eyelids sink? I find Not myself disposed to sleep.
Antonio	Nor I. My spirits are nimble. They fell together all, as by consent They dropped, as by a thunder-stroke. What might, Worthy Sebastian? O, what might? No more. 185 And yet, methinks I see it in thy face, What thou shouldst be. Th'occasion speaks thee, and My strong imagination sees a crown Dropping upon thy head.
Sebastian	What? Art thou waking?
Antonio	Do you not hear me speak?
Sebastian	I do, and surely 190 It is a sleepy language and thou speak'st Out of thy sleep. What is it thou didst say? This is a strange repose, to be asleep With eyes wide open. Standing, speaking, moving, And yet so fast asleep.
Antonio	Noble Sebastian, 195 Thou let'st thy fortune sleep – die, rather. Wink'st Whiles thou art waking.
Sebastian	Thou dost snore distinctly. There's meaning in thy snores.
Antonio	I am more serious than my custom. You Must be so too, if heed me; which to do 200 Trebles thee o'er.
Sebastian	Well; I am standing water.
Antonio	I'll teach you how to flow.

Antonio continues to encourage Sebastian's ambition to become King of Naples by saying that Ferdinand must have drowned and Claribel, as next in line to the throne, is too far away.

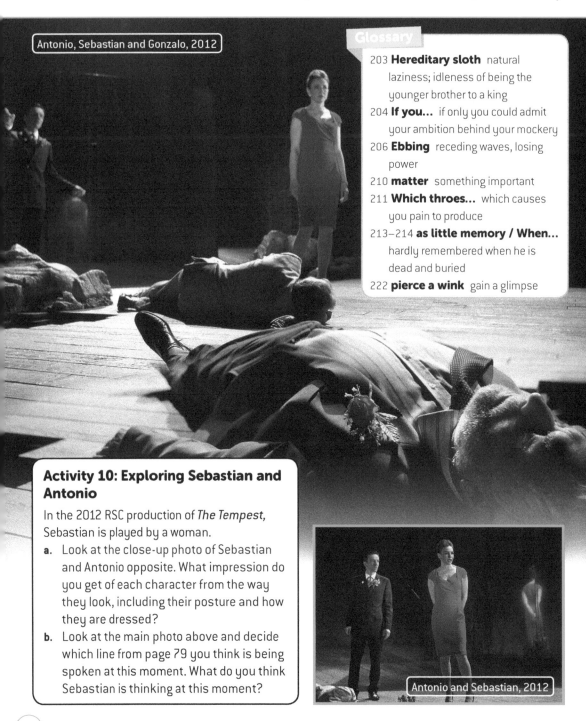

Antonio, Sebastian and Gonzalo, 2012

Glossary

203 **Hereditary sloth** natural laziness; idleness of being the younger brother to a king

204 **If you...** if only you could admit your ambition behind your mockery

206 **Ebbing** receding waves, losing power

210 **matter** something important

211 **Which throes...** which causes you pain to produce

213–214 **as little memory / When...** hardly remembered when he is dead and buried

222 **pierce a wink** gain a glimpse

Activity 10: Exploring Sebastian and Antonio

In the 2012 RSC production of *The Tempest*, Sebastian is played by a woman.

a. Look at the close-up photo of Sebastian and Antonio opposite. What impression do you get of each character from the way they look, including their posture and how they are dressed?

b. Look at the main photo above and decide which line from page 79 you think is being spoken at this moment. What do you think Sebastian is thinking at this moment?

Antonio and Sebastian, 2012

Sebastian	Do so. To ebb
	Hereditary sloth instructs me.
Antonio	O!
	If you but knew how you the purpose cherish
	Whiles thus you mock it; how in stripping it 205
	You more invest it. Ebbing men, indeed,
	Most often, do so near the bottom run
	By their own fear, or sloth.
Sebastian	Prithee, say on.
	The setting of thine eye and cheek proclaim
	A matter from thee; and a birth, indeed, 210
	Which throes thee much to yield.
Antonio	Thus, sir;
	Although this lord of weak remembrance, this,
	Who shall be of as little memory
	When he is earthed, hath here almost persuaded –
	For he's a spirit of persuasion, only 215
	Professes to persuade – the king his son's alive,
	'Tis as impossible that he's undrowned
	As he that sleeps here swims.
Sebastian	I have no hope
	That he's undrowned.
Antonio	O, out of that 'no hope'
	What great hope have you? No hope that way is 220
	Another way so high a hope, that even
	Ambition cannot pierce a wink beyond
	But doubt discovery there. Will you grant with me
	That Ferdinand is drowned?
Sebastian	He's gone.
Antonio	Then, tell me, who's the next heir of Naples?
Sebastian	Claribel. 225
Antonio	She that is Queen of Tunis. She that dwells
	Ten leagues beyond man's life. She that from Naples

Antonio emphasises further that Claribel is too far away in Tunis to rule Naples and tells Sebastian that he should rule instead. Sebastian remembers that Antonio stole the dukedom of Milan from his own brother Prospero, and Antonio says he has done very well from it.

Activity 11: Exploring the relationship between Sebastian and Antonio

a. In groups, read aloud lines 237–255, swapping reader at each punctuation mark.
b. Discuss what you think Sebastian might be thinking during this exchange.
c. Imagine you are Sebastian and list all the reasons you can think of for killing Alonso and all the reasons you can think of against killing him. Look at the 'At the time' task to help you.
d. One of you plays Sebastian and the others in your group take sides to argue, in your own words, either for or against killing Alonso. 'Sebastian' calls 'stop' when he knows no further arguments will convince him one way or the other.
e. Swap round so that others in your group play Sebastian.
f. Discuss how the 'Sebastians' felt, and which arguments they found most convincing and why.
g. Write a paragraph summarising why you think Sebastian agrees to Antonio's plan.

Glossary

231 **cast again** castaways on the island; cast in new roles
234 **In yours and my discharge** in our powers to perform
237 **cubit** a measurement of about 20 inches
243 **prate** prattle
245 **I myself could make...** I could train a jackdaw to speak as Gonzalo does
253 **feater** better fitting

At the time

Using page 187, find out more about attitudes to kingship and succession in Shakespeare's time. Using this information, discuss what audiences in Shakespeare's time might have thought about Antonio's ideas.

Alonso (on the ground), Antonio, Sebastian and Gonzalo (on the ground), 2016

Can have no note, unless the sun were post –
The man i'th'moon's too slow – till new-born chins
Be rough and razorable. She that from whom   230
We all were sea-swallowed, though some cast again –
And by that destiny – to perform an act
Whereof what's past is prologue, what to come
In yours and my discharge.

Sebastian   What stuff is this? How say you?
'Tis true, my brother's daughter's Queen of Tunis.   235
So is she heir of Naples, 'twixt which regions
There is some space.

Antonio   A space whose every cubit
Seems to cry out, 'How shall that Claribel
Measure us back to Naples? Keep in Tunis,
And let Sebastian wake.' Say this were death   240
That now hath seized them. Why, they were no worse
Than now they are. There be that can rule Naples
As well as he that sleeps. Lords that can prate
As amply and unnecessarily
As this Gonzalo. I myself could make   245
A chough of as deep chat. O, that you bore
The mind that I do, what a sleep were this
For your advancement. Do you understand me?

Sebastian   Methinks I do.

Antonio   And how does your content
Tender your own good fortune?

Sebastian   I remember   250
You did supplant your brother Prospero.

Antonio   True,
And look how well my garments sit upon me,
Much feater than before. My brother's servants
Were then my fellows. Now they are my men.

Sebastian   But for your conscience.   255

Antonio says his conscience doesn't bother him over how he treated Prospero and encourages Sebastian to kill Gonzalo at the same time as he kills Alonso. Sebastian agrees and both raise their swords. Sebastian hesitates and in this moment Ariel wakes up Gonzalo.

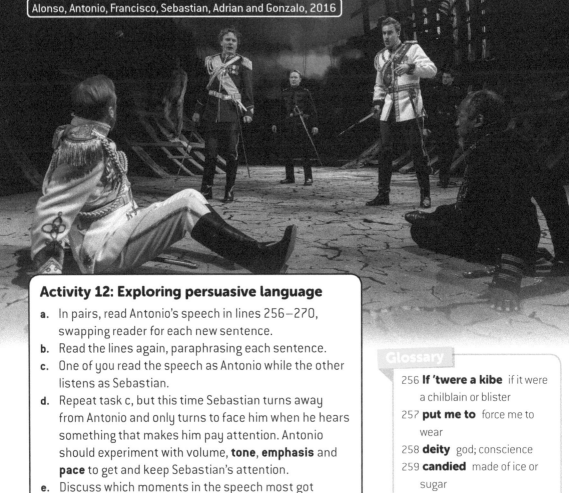

Alonso, Antonio, Francisco, Sebastian, Adrian and Gonzalo, 2016

Activity 12: Exploring persuasive language

a. In pairs, read Antonio's speech in lines 256–270, swapping reader for each new sentence.

b. Read the lines again, paraphrasing each sentence.

c. One of you read the speech as Antonio while the other listens as Sebastian.

d. Repeat task c, but this time Sebastian turns away from Antonio and only turns to face him when he hears something that makes him pay attention. Antonio should experiment with volume, **tone**, **emphasis** and **pace** to get and keep Sebastian's attention.

e. Discuss which moments in the speech most got Sebastian's attention. Why do you think Antonio suggests that Sebastian kill Gonzalo?

Glossary

256 **If 'twere a kibe** if it were a chilblain or blister

257 **put me to** force me to wear

258 **deity** god; conscience

259 **candied** made of ice or sugar

265 **perpetual wink for aye** endless sleep for ever

266 **ancient morsel** old flesh, i.e. Gonzalo

273 **tribute** payment from Milan to Naples agreed by Antonio in exchange for Alonso's help in usurping Prospero

Key terms

Tone as in 'tone of voice'; expressing an attitude through how you say something

Emphasis stress given to words when speaking

Pace the speed at which someone speaks

Antonio   Ay, sir, where lies that? If 'twere a kibe,
                'Twould put me to my slipper; but I feel not
                This deity in my bosom. Twenty consciences
                That stand 'twixt me and Milan, candied be they,
                And melt ere they molest. Here lies your brother,   260
                No better than the earth he lies upon,
                If he were that which now he's like – that's dead –
                Whom I with this obedient steel – three inches of it –
                Can lay to bed forever. Whiles you, doing thus,
                To the perpetual wink for aye might put   265
                This ancient morsel, this Sir Prudence, who
                Should not upbraid our course. For all the rest,
                They'll take suggestion as a cat laps milk.
                They'll tell the clock to any business that
                We say befits the hour.

Sebastian   Thy case, dear friend,   270
                Shall be my precedent. As thou got'st Milan,
                I'll come by Naples. Draw thy sword. One stroke
                Shall free thee from the tribute which thou payest,
                And I the king shall love thee.

Antonio   Draw together.
                And when I rear my hand, do you the like,   275
                To fall it on Gonzalo.

Sebastian   O, but one word.

Enter Ariel, invisible, with music and song

Ariel   My master through his art foresees the danger
                That you, his friend, are in, and sends me forth,
                For else his project dies, to keep them living.

Sings in Gonzalo's ear

                While you here do snoring lie,   280
                Open-eyed conspiracy
                His time doth take.
                If of life you keep a care,
                Shake off slumber, and beware.
                Awake, awake!   285

Gonzalo wakes up and shouts out, waking the others. Sebastian and Antonio pretend their swords are drawn because they heard a strange noise. They all agree to carry on looking for Ferdinand.

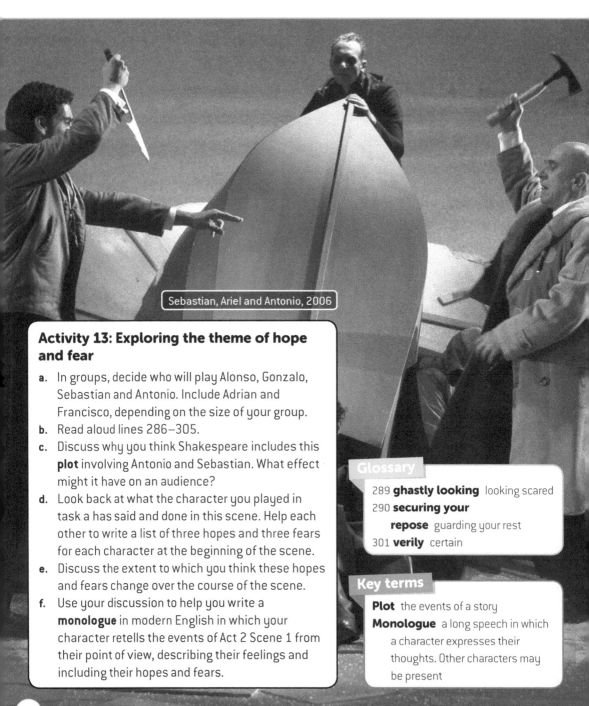

Sebastian, Ariel and Antonio, 2006

Activity 13: Exploring the theme of hope and fear

a. In groups, decide who will play Alonso, Gonzalo, Sebastian and Antonio. Include Adrian and Francisco, depending on the size of your group.

b. Read aloud lines 286–305.

c. Discuss why you think Shakespeare includes this **plot** involving Antonio and Sebastian. What effect might it have on an audience?

d. Look back at what the character you played in task a has said and done in this scene. Help each other to write a list of three hopes and three fears for each character at the beginning of the scene.

e. Discuss the extent to which you think these hopes and fears change over the course of the scene.

f. Use your discussion to help you write a **monologue** in modern English in which your character retells the events of Act 2 Scene 1 from their point of view, describing their feelings and including their hopes and fears.

Glossary

289 **ghastly looking** looking scared
290 **securing your**
     repose guarding your rest
301 **verily** certain

Key terms

Plot the events of a story
Monologue a long speech in which a character expresses their thoughts. Other characters may be present

Antonio	Then let us both be sudden.

| Gonzalo | [Waking] Now, good angels |

Preserve the king!

The others wake

Alonso	Why, how now, ho. Awake? Why are you drawn?

Wherefore this ghastly looking?

| Gonzalo | What's the matter? |

Sebastian	Whiles we stood here securing your repose,	290

Even now, we heard a hollow burst of bellowing
Like bulls, or rather lions. Did't not wake you?
It struck mine ear most terribly.

| Alonso | I heard nothing. |

Antonio	O, 'twas a din to fright a monster's ear,

To make an earthquake. Sure it was the roar   295
Of a whole herd of lions.

| Alonso | Heard you this, Gonzalo? |

Gonzalo	Upon mine honour, sir, I heard a humming,

And that a strange one too, which did awake me.
I shaked you, sir, and cried. As mine eyes opened,
I saw their weapons drawn. There was a noise,   300
That's verily. 'Tis best we stand upon our guard,
Or that we quit this place. Let's draw our weapons.

Alonso	Lead off this ground, and let's make further search

For my poor son.

| Gonzalo | Heavens keep him from these beasts; |

For he is sure i'th'island.

| Alonso | Lead away. | 305 |

Ariel	Prospero, my lord, shall know what I have done.

So, king, go safely on to seek thy son.

Exeunt

Caliban curses Prospero, then worries that Prospero's spirits might punish him. He sees Trinculo approaching, thinks he might be one of the spirits and so hides. Trinculo is looking for somewhere to shelter from the oncoming storm. He sees Caliban and thinks he smells like a fish.

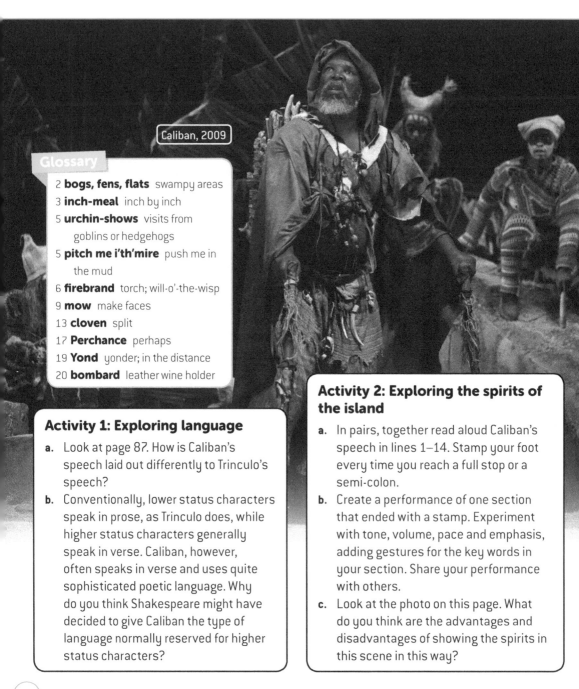

Caliban, 2009

Glossary

2 **bogs, fens, flats** swampy areas

3 **inch-meal** inch by inch

5 **urchin-shows** visits from goblins or hedgehogs

5 **pitch me i'th'mire** push me in the mud

6 **firebrand** torch; will-o'-the-wisp

9 **mow** make faces

13 **cloven** split

17 **Perchance** perhaps

19 **Yond** yonder; in the distance

20 **bombard** leather wine holder

Activity 1: Exploring language

a. Look at page 87. How is Caliban's speech laid out differently to Trinculo's speech?

b. Conventionally, lower status characters speak in prose, as Trinculo does, while higher status characters generally speak in verse. Caliban, however, often speaks in verse and uses quite sophisticated poetic language. Why do you think Shakespeare might have decided to give Caliban the type of language normally reserved for higher status characters?

Activity 2: Exploring the spirits of the island

a. In pairs, together read aloud Caliban's speech in lines 1–14. Stamp your foot every time you reach a full stop or a semi-colon.

b. Create a performance of one section that ended with a stamp. Experiment with tone, volume, pace and emphasis, adding gestures for the key words in your section. Share your performance with others.

c. Look at the photo on this page. What do you think are the advantages and disadvantages of showing the spirits in this scene in this way?

Act 2 | Scene 2

Caliban   All the infections that the sun sucks up
From bogs, fens, flats, on Prosper fall, and make him
By inch-meal a disease. His spirits hear me,
And yet I needs must curse. But they'll nor pinch,
Fright me with urchin-shows, pitch me i'th'mire,   5
Nor lead me like a firebrand in the dark
Out of my way, unless he bid 'em; but
For every trifle are they set upon me,
Sometime like apes, that mow and chatter at me,
And after bite me; then like hedgehogs, which   10
Lie tumbling in my barefoot way and mount
Their pricks at my footfall. Sometime am I
All wound with adders, who with cloven tongues
Do hiss me into madness.

                    Lo, now, lo,
Here comes a spirit of his, and to torment me   15
For bringing wood in slowly. I'll fall flat,
Perchance he will not mind me.

Trinculo   Here's neither bush nor shrub to bear off any weather at all, and
another storm brewing. I hear it sing i'th'wind. Yond same black
cloud, yond huge one, looks like a foul bombard that would shed   20
his liquor. If it should thunder as it did before, I know not where to
hide my head. Yond same cloud cannot choose but fall by pailfuls.
[Seeing Caliban] What have we here? A man or a fish? Dead or
alive? A fish, he smells like a fish – a very ancient and fishlike

Trinculo crawls under Caliban's cloak to shelter from the rain. Stephano enters singing and drinking wine from a bottle. Stephano notices a strange creature that seems to have four legs.

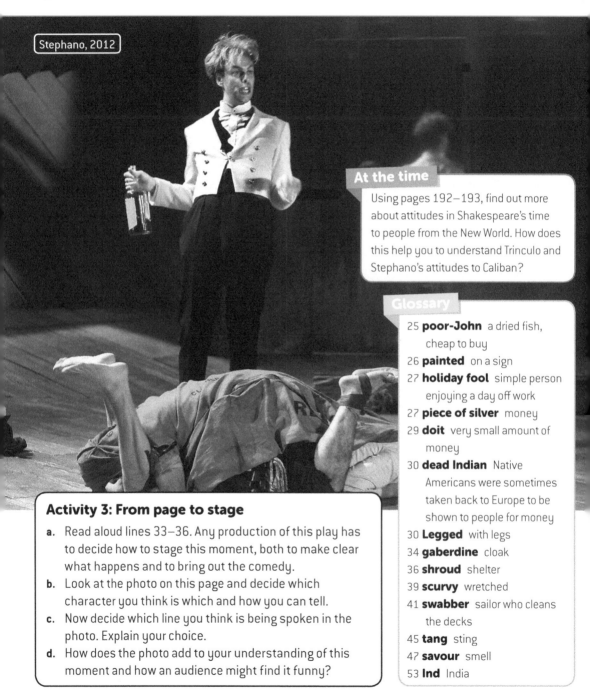

Stephano, 2012

At the time

Using pages 192–193, find out more about attitudes in Shakespeare's time to people from the New World. How does this help you to understand Trinculo and Stephano's attitudes to Caliban?

Glossary

25 **poor-John** a dried fish, cheap to buy
26 **painted** on a sign
27 **holiday fool** simple person enjoying a day off work
27 **piece of silver** money
29 **doit** very small amount of money
30 **dead Indian** Native Americans were sometimes taken back to Europe to be shown to people for money
30 **Legged** with legs
34 **gaberdine** cloak
36 **shroud** shelter
39 **scurvy** wretched
41 **swabber** sailor who cleans the decks
45 **tang** sting
47 **savour** smell
53 **Ind** India

Activity 3: From page to stage

a. Read aloud lines 33–36. Any production of this play has to decide how to stage this moment, both to make clear what happens and to bring out the comedy.
b. Look at the photo on this page and decide which character you think is which and how you can tell.
c. Now decide which line you think is being spoken in the photo. Explain your choice.
d. How does the photo add to your understanding of this moment and how an audience might find it funny?

smell; a kind of not-of-the-newest poor-John. A strange fish. Were   25
I in England now, as once I was, and had but this fish painted, not
a holiday fool there but would give a piece of silver. There would
this monster make a man. Any strange beast there makes a man.
When they will not give a doit to relieve a lame beggar, they will
lay out ten to see a dead Indian. Legged like a man and his fins   30
like arms. Warm, o'my troth. I do now let loose my opinion, hold
it no longer, this is no fish, but an islander that hath lately suffered
by a thunderbolt. [Thunder] Alas, the storm is come again. My
best way is to creep under his gaberdine. There is no other shelter
hereabout. Misery acquaints a man with strange bedfellows. I will   35
here shroud till the dregs of the storm be past.

*He hides under Caliban's cloak. Enter Stephano with a bottle in his
hand, singing*

Stephano   I shall no more to sea, to sea,
Here shall I die ashore.
This is a very scurvy tune to sing at a man's funeral. Well, here's
my comfort.   40

Stephano drinks from a bottle

[Sings] The master, the swabber, the boatswain and I,
The gunner and his mate,
Loved Moll, Meg and Marian and Margery,
But none of us cared for Kate.
For she had a tongue with a tang,   45
Would cry to a sailor, 'Go hang!'
She loved not the savour of tar nor of pitch,
Yet a tailor might scratch her where'er she did itch.
Then to sea, boys, and let her go hang.
This is a scurvy tune too: but here's my comfort.   50

He drinks again

Caliban   Do not torment me. O!

Stephano   What's the matter? Have we devils here? Do you put tricks upon's
with savages and men of Ind, ha? I have not 'scaped drowning to
be afeard now of your four legs. For it hath been said, 'As proper

Stephano thinks he has found a strange native of the island and gives him alcohol from his bottle. Stephano intends to subdue Caliban and take him back to Europe to make money from him. Trinculo recognises Stephano's voice and calls out to him.

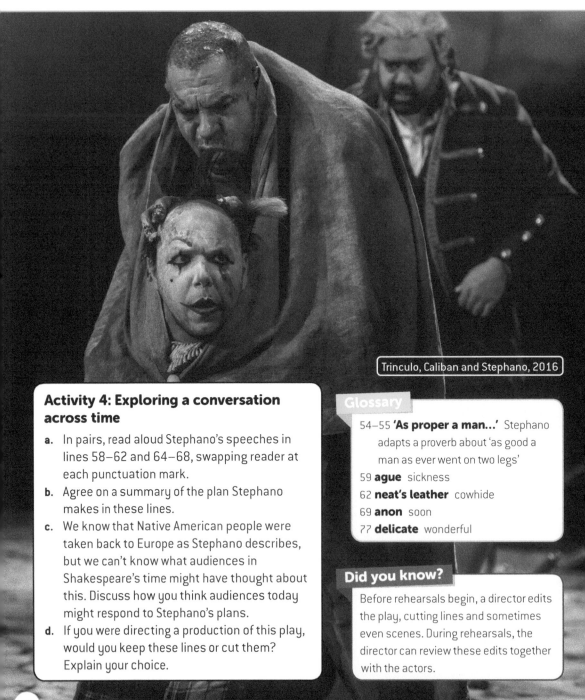

Trinculo, Caliban and Stephano, 2016

Activity 4: Exploring a conversation across time

a. In pairs, read aloud Stephano's speeches in lines 58–62 and 64–68, swapping reader at each punctuation mark.

b. Agree on a summary of the plan Stephano makes in these lines.

c. We know that Native American people were taken back to Europe as Stephano describes, but we can't know what audiences in Shakespeare's time might have thought about this. Discuss how you think audiences today might respond to Stephano's plans.

d. If you were directing a production of this play, would you keep these lines or cut them? Explain your choice.

Glossary

54–55 **'As proper a man...'** Stephano adapts a proverb about 'as good a man as ever went on two legs'

59 **ague** sickness

62 **neat's leather** cowhide

69 **anon** soon

77 **delicate** wonderful

Did you know?

Before rehearsals begin, a director edits the play, cutting lines and sometimes even scenes. During rehearsals, the director can review these edits together with the actors.

a man as ever went on four legs, cannot make him give ground'; 55
and it shall be said so again, while Stephano breathes at'nostrils.

Caliban The spirit torments me. O!

Stephano This is some monster of the isle with four legs, who hath got, as I
take it, an ague. Where the devil should he learn our language? I
will give him some relief, if it be but for that. If I can recover him, 60
and keep him tame, and get to Naples with him, he's a present for
any emperor that ever trod on neat's leather.

Caliban Do not torment me, prithee. I'll bring my wood home faster.

Stephano He's in his fit now, and does not talk after the wisest. He shall taste
of my bottle. If he have never drunk wine afore, it will go near to 65
remove his fit. If I can recover him and keep him tame, I will not
take too much for him. He shall pay for him that hath him, and
that soundly.

Caliban Thou dost me yet but little hurt. Thou wilt anon, I know it by thy
trembling. Now Prosper works upon thee. 70

Stephano Come on your ways. Open your mouth. Here is that which will
give language to you, cat. Open your mouth. This will shake your
shaking, I can tell you, and that soundly.

Caliban drinks

You cannot tell who's your friend. Open your chaps again.

Caliban drinks again

Trinculo I should know that voice. It should be – but he is drowned, and 75
these are devils. O, defend me!

Stephano Four legs and two voices – a most delicate monster! His forward
voice now is to speak well of his friend, his backward voice is to
utter foul speeches and to detract. If all the wine in my bottle will
recover him, I will help his ague. Come. 80

Caliban drinks

Amen. I will pour some in thy other mouth.

Trinculo Stephano!

Stephano pulls Trinculo out from Caliban's cloak and they discuss how they survived the shipwreck. Caliban thinks Stephano is a god because of the wine he brings.

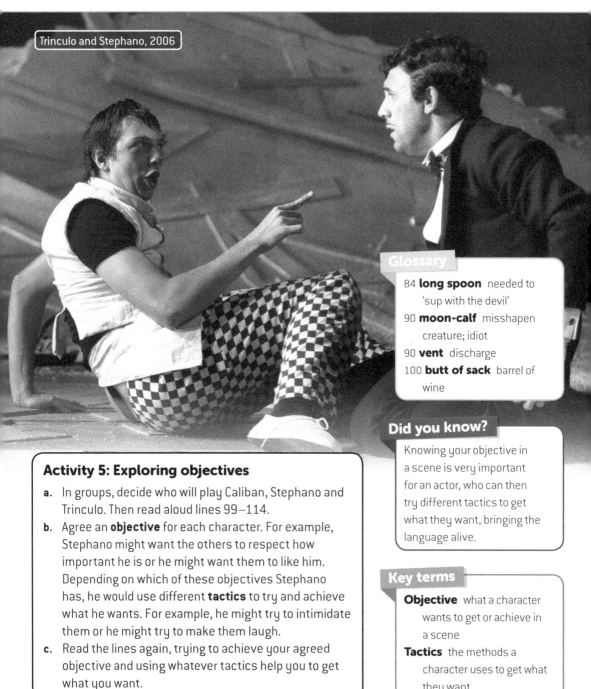

Trinculo and Stephano, 2006

Glossary

84 **long spoon** needed to 'sup with the devil'

90 **moon-calf** misshapen creature; idiot

90 **vent** discharge

100 **butt of sack** barrel of wine

Did you know?

Knowing your objective in a scene is very important for an actor, who can then try different tactics to get what they want, bringing the language alive.

Key terms

Objective what a character wants to get or achieve in a scene

Tactics the methods a character uses to get what they want

Activity 5: Exploring objectives

a. In groups, decide who will play Caliban, Stephano and Trinculo. Then read aloud lines 99–114.

b. Agree an **objective** for each character. For example, Stephano might want the others to respect how important he is or he might want them to like him. Depending on which of these objectives Stephano has, he would use different **tactics** to try and achieve what he wants. For example, he might try to intimidate them or he might try to make them laugh.

c. Read the lines again, trying to achieve your agreed objective and using whatever tactics help you to get what you want.

Stephano	Doth thy other mouth call me? Mercy, mercy! This is a devil, and no monster. I will leave him, I have no long spoon.
Trinculo	Stephano! If thou beest Stephano, touch me and speak to me. For I am Trinculo, be not afeard, thy good friend Trinculo.
Stephano	If thou beest Trinculo, come forth. I'll pull thee by the lesser legs. If any be Trinculo's legs, these are they. [He pulls out Trinculo by the legs] Thou art very Trinculo indeed! How cam'st thou to be the siege of this moon-calf? Can he vent Trinculos?
Trinculo	I took him to be killed with a thunder-stroke. But art thou not drowned, Stephano? I hope now thou art not drowned. Is the storm overblown? I hid me under the dead moon-calf's gaberdine for fear of the storm. And art thou living, Stephano? O Stephano, two Neapolitans 'scaped?
Stephano	Prithee, do not turn me about. My stomach is not constant.
Caliban	[Aside] These be fine things, and if they be not sprites. That's a brave god and bears celestial liquor. I will kneel to him.
Stephano	How didst thou 'scape? How cam'st thou hither? Swear by this bottle how thou cam'st hither. I escaped upon a butt of sack which the sailors heaved o'erboard — by this bottle which I made of the bark of a tree with mine own hands since I was cast ashore.
Caliban	I'll swear upon that bottle to be thy true subject, for the liquor is not earthly.
Stephano	Here. Swear then how thou escap'dst.
Trinculo	Swum ashore, man, like a duck. I can swim like a duck, I'll be sworn.
Stephano	Here, kiss the book. [Trinculo drinks] Though thou canst swim like a duck, thou art made like a goose.
Trinculo	O Stephano, hast any more of this?
Stephano	The whole butt, man. My cellar is in a rock by the sea-side, where my wine is hid. [To Caliban] How now, moon-calf? How does thine ague?
Caliban	Hast thou not dropped from heaven?

85

90

95

100

105

110

Caliban offers his services to Stephano as his new master instead of Prospero. Trinculo ridicules Caliban.

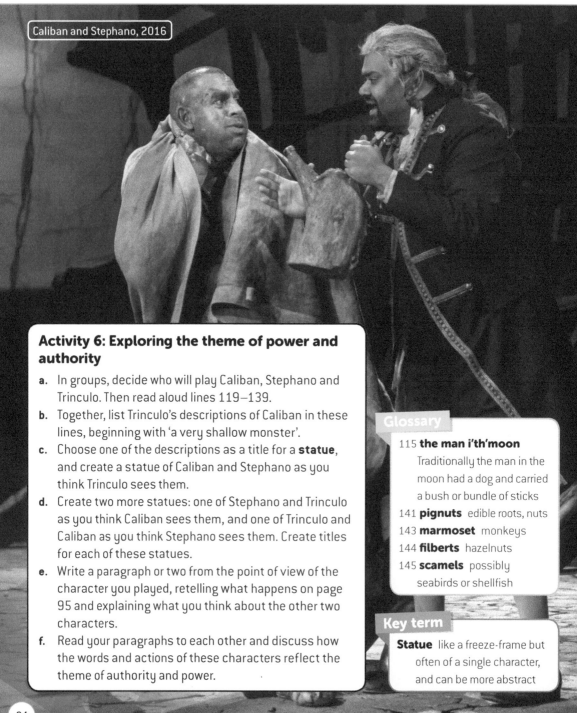

Caliban and Stephano, 2016

Activity 6: Exploring the theme of power and authority

a. In groups, decide who will play Caliban, Stephano and Trinculo. Then read aloud lines 119–139.

b. Together, list Trinculo's descriptions of Caliban in these lines, beginning with 'a very shallow monster'.

c. Choose one of the descriptions as a title for a **statue**, and create a statue of Caliban and Stephano as you think Trinculo sees them.

d. Create two more statues: one of Stephano and Trinculo as you think Caliban sees them, and one of Trinculo and Caliban as you think Stephano sees them. Create titles for each of these statues.

e. Write a paragraph or two from the point of view of the character you played, retelling what happens on page 95 and explaining what you think about the other two characters.

f. Read your paragraphs to each other and discuss how the words and actions of these characters reflect the theme of authority and power.

Glossary

115 **the man i'th'moon**
Traditionally the man in the moon had a dog and carried a bush or bundle of sticks

141 **pignuts** edible roots, nuts

143 **marmoset** monkeys

144 **filberts** hazelnuts

145 **scamels** possibly seabirds or shellfish

Key term

Statue like a freeze-frame but often of a single character, and can be more abstract

Stephano	Out o'th'moon, I do assure thee. I was the man i'th'moon when 115 time was.
Caliban	I have seen thee in her, and I do adore thee. My mistress showed me thee, and thy dog, and thy bush.
Stephano	Come, swear to that. Kiss the book. I will furnish it anon with new contents. Swear. 120
	Caliban drinks
Trinculo	By this good light, this is a very shallow monster. I afeard of him? A very weak monster. The man i'th'moon? A most poor, credulous monster. Well drawn, monster, in good sooth.
Caliban	I'll show thee every fertile inch o'th'island; And I will kiss thy foot. I prithee, be my god. 125
Trinculo	By this light, a most perfidious and drunken monster. When's god's asleep, he'll rob his bottle.
Caliban	I'll kiss thy foot. I'll swear myself thy subject.
Stephano	Come on then. Down, and swear.
Trinculo	I shall laugh myself to death at this puppy-headed monster. 130 A most scurvy monster. I could find in my heart to beat him.
Stephano	[To Caliban] Come, kiss.
Trinculo	But that the poor monster's in drink. An abominable monster.
Caliban	I'll show thee the best springs. I'll pluck thee berries. I'll fish for thee and get thee wood enough. 135 A plague upon the tyrant that I serve! I'll bear him no more sticks, but follow thee, Thou wondrous man.
Trinculo	A most ridiculous monster, to make a wonder of a poor drunkard.
Caliban	I prithee, let me bring thee where crabs grow; 140 And I with my long nails will dig thee pignuts; Show thee a jay's nest, and instruct thee how To snare the nimble marmoset. I'll bring thee To clustering filberts, and sometimes I'll get thee Young scamels from the rock. Wilt thou go with me? 145

Stephano is pleased to be worshipped by Caliban and Caliban is delighted to have a new master.

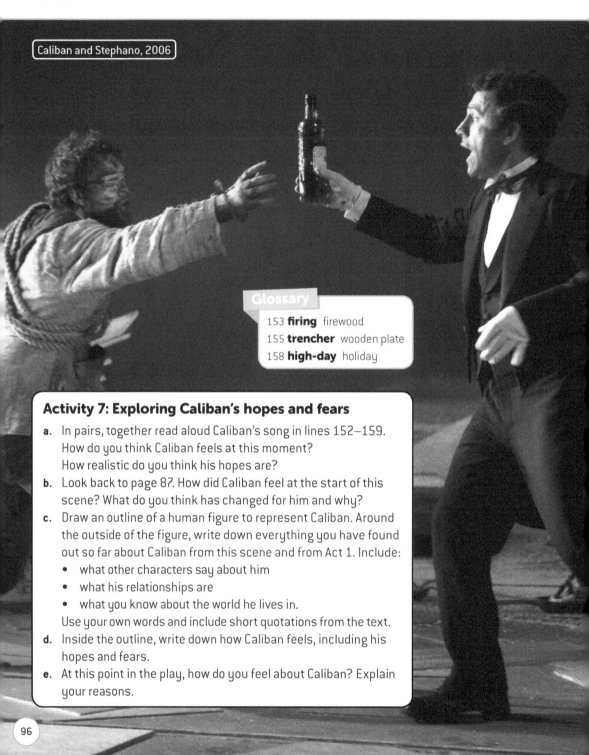

Caliban and Stephano, 2006

Glossary

153 **firing** firewood
155 **trencher** wooden plate
158 **high-day** holiday

Activity 7: Exploring Caliban's hopes and fears

a. In pairs, together read aloud Caliban's song in lines 152–159.
   How do you think Caliban feels at this moment?
   How realistic do you think his hopes are?
b. Look back to page 87. How did Caliban feel at the start of this scene? What do you think has changed for him and why?
c. Draw an outline of a human figure to represent Caliban. Around the outside of the figure, write down everything you have found out so far about Caliban from this scene and from Act 1. Include:
   • what other characters say about him
   • what his relationships are
   • what you know about the world he lives in.
   Use your own words and include short quotations from the text.
d. Inside the outline, write down how Caliban feels, including his hopes and fears.
e. At this point in the play, how do you feel about Caliban? Explain your reasons.

Stephano	I prithee, now lead the way without any more talking. Trinculo, the king and all our company else being drowned, we will inherit here. [To Caliban] Here, bear my bottle. Fellow Trinculo, we'll fill him by and by again.
Caliban	[Sings drunkenly] Farewell master! Farewell, farewell.

150

Trinculo	A howling monster. A drunken monster.
Caliban	[Sings] No more dams I'll make for fish,

        Nor fetch in firing
        At requiring,
        Nor scrape trencher, nor wash dish,

155

        Ban, ban, Cacaliban
        Has a new master. Get a new man.
Freedom, high-day! High-day, freedom! Freedom,
high-day, freedom!

Stephano	O brave monster, lead the way.

160

[Exeunt]

Exploring Act 2

Prospero and Ariel, 2006

Activity 1: Exploring the development of themes in Act 2

a. In pairs, look back through Act 2 and rank the following themes in order of their importance for the two scenes in this Act (the highest should be ranked 1; the lowest 4):
   - Authority and power
   - Hope and fear
   - Family
   - Vengeance and forgiveness.
b. Join with another pair and compare your rank order with theirs. Discuss any differences.
c. As a group, choose one theme and create a presentation in which you argue for the importance of your theme in this Act.

Activity 2: Ariel's report

Look back at line 306 on page 85 where Ariel says to the audience 'Prospero, my lord, shall know what I have done.' Look back through Act 2 Scene 1, noting everything Ariel has done and everything he has seen and heard. Write a short monologue for Ariel in which he reports back to Prospero on what has happened in this scene. Try to write in a style you think would be appropriate for Ariel and consider what sort of words and phrases Ariel might use to describe the events.

Ferdinand is piling up logs and says he is happy to do it as long as Miranda is nearby. She enters and asks him to rest. Prospero watches them without being seen.

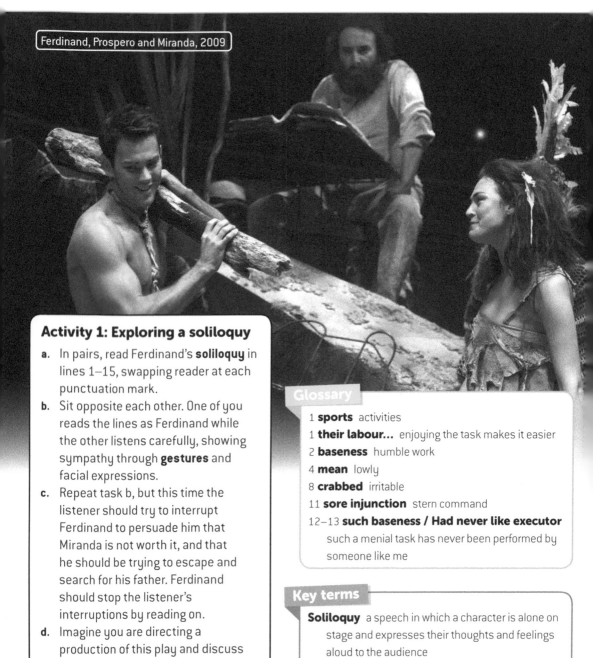

Ferdinand, Prospero and Miranda, 2009

Activity 1: Exploring a soliloquy

a. In pairs, read Ferdinand's **soliloquy** in lines 1–15, swapping reader at each punctuation mark.

b. Sit opposite each other. One of you reads the lines as Ferdinand while the other listens carefully, showing sympathy through **gestures** and facial expressions.

c. Repeat task b, but this time the listener should try to interrupt Ferdinand to persuade him that Miranda is not worth it, and that he should be trying to escape and search for his father. Ferdinand should stop the listener's interruptions by reading on.

d. Imagine you are directing a production of this play and discuss how you would want the audience to feel about Ferdinand at this moment.

Glossary

1 **sports** activities
1 **their labour...** enjoying the task makes it easier
2 **baseness** humble work
4 **mean** lowly
8 **crabbed** irritable
11 **sore injunction** stern command
12–13 **such baseness / Had never like executor** such a menial task has never been performed by someone like me

Key terms

Soliloquy a speech in which a character is alone on stage and expresses their thoughts and feelings aloud to the audience

Gesture a movement, often using the hands or head, to express a feeling or idea

Act 3 | Scene 1

Ferdinand   There be some sports are painful, and their labour
Delight in them sets off. Some kinds of baseness
Are nobly undergone, and most poor matters
Point to rich ends. This my mean task
Would be as heavy to me as odious, but   5
The mistress which I serve quickens what's dead
And makes my labours pleasures. O, she is
Ten times more gentle than her father's crabbed,
And he's composed of harshness. I must remove
Some thousands of these logs and pile them up,   10
Upon a sore injunction. My sweet mistress
Weeps when she sees me work and says such baseness
Had never like executor. I forget.
But these sweet thoughts do even refresh my labours,
Most busy least, when I do it.

Enter Miranda, and Prospero following at a distance unseen

Miranda   Alas, now pray you,   15
Work not so hard. I would the lightning had
Burnt up those logs that you are enjoined to pile.
Pray, set it down and rest you. When this burns
'Twill weep for having wearied you. My father
Is hard at study. Pray now, rest yourself,   20
He's safe for these three hours.

Ferdinand   O most dear mistress,
The sun will set before I shall discharge
What I must strive to do.

Miranda   If you'll sit down,
I'll bear your logs the while. Pray give me that,
I'll carry it to the pile.

Miranda offers to help Ferdinand but he thinks this would be dishonourable. He asks her name and she tells him, although her father had told her not to. He tells her she is perfect.

Glossary

31 **infected** with love
37 **hest** command
46 **put it to the foil** put it to the sword; defeat it
50 **glass** mirror

Ferdinand, Miranda and Prospero, 2012

Key terms

Iambic pentameter the rhythm Shakespeare uses to write his plays. Each line in this rhythm contains approximately ten **syllables**. 'Iambic' means putting the stress on the second syllable of each beat. 'Pentameter' means five beats with two syllables in each beat

Shared lines lines of iambic pentameter shared between characters. This implies a closeness between them in some way

Tone as in 'tone of voice'; expressing an attitude through how you say something

Emphasis stress given to words when speaking

Pace the speed at which someone speaks

Syllable part of a word that is one sound, e.g. 'tempest' has two syllables 'tem' and 'pest'

Activity 2: Exploring Miranda and Ferdinand's relationship

a. In pairs, decide who will play Ferdinand and who will play Miranda. Then read aloud lines 15–31.

b. Read the lines again, fitting them to the **iambic pentameter** rhythm (see page 24).

c. What do you think is the effect of Ferdinand and Miranda's **shared lines**, when they share the rhythm across their lines?

d. Experiment with reading the lines again, with an awareness of the rhythm but using **tone**, **emphasis** and **pace** as seems appropriate.

e. Look at the 'Did you know?' box on this page and discuss what action you think should happen about the logs.

f. Create a performance of this exchange, adding in all your ideas from the tasks in this activity.

Did you know?

In some productions of this play, there is often a visual joke that Miranda picks up and easily carries a log that Ferdinand has struggled with.

At the time

Using pages 194–196, find out more about the women Ferdinand is used to meeting and discuss how different Miranda might seem to him and why.

Ferdinand	No, precious creature, 25
	I had rather crack my sinews, break my back,
	Than you should such dishonour undergo,
	While I sit lazy by.
Miranda	It would become me
	As well as it does you; and I should do it
	With much more ease, for my good will is to it, 30
	And yours it is against.
Prospero	[Aside] Poor worm, thou art infected.
	This visitation shows it.
Miranda	You look wearily.
Ferdinand	No, noble mistress, 'tis fresh morning with me
	When you are by at night. I do beseech you,
	Chiefly that I might set it in my prayers, 35
	What is your name?
Miranda	Miranda. O my father,
	I have broke your hest to say so.
Ferdinand	Admired Miranda,
	Indeed the top of admiration, worth
	What's dearest to the world. Full many a lady
	I have eyed with best regard, and many a time 40
	The harmony of their tongues hath into bondage
	Brought my too diligent ear. For several virtues
	Have I liked several women, never any
	With so full soul but some defect in her
	Did quarrel with the noblest grace she owed, 45
	And put it to the foil. But you, O you,
	So perfect and so peerless, are created
	Of every creature's best.
Miranda	I do not know
	One of my sex; no woman's face remember,
	Save from my glass, mine own. Nor have I seen 50
	More that I may call men than you, good friend,
	And my dear father. How features are abroad,

Ferdinand tells Miranda he is a prince, probably a king, but is happy to endure being a slave carrying logs for her sake because he loves her. Prospero is secretly delighted as he watches them declare their love for each other.

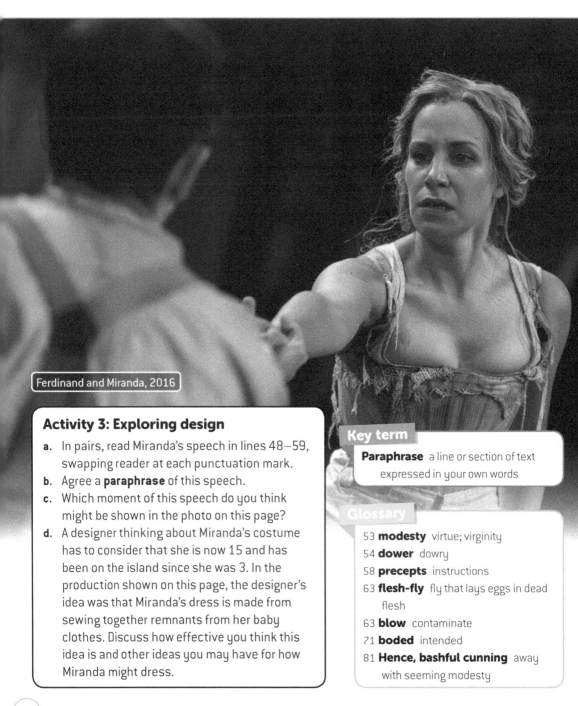

Ferdinand and Miranda, 2016

Activity 3: Exploring design

a. In pairs, read Miranda's speech in lines 48–59, swapping reader at each punctuation mark.
b. Agree a **paraphrase** of this speech.
c. Which moment of this speech do you think might be shown in the photo on this page?
d. A designer thinking about Miranda's costume has to consider that she is now 15 and has been on the island since she was 3. In the production shown on this page, the designer's idea was that Miranda's dress is made from sewing together remnants from her baby clothes. Discuss how effective you think this idea is and other ideas you may have for how Miranda might dress.

Key term

Paraphrase a line or section of text expressed in your own words

Glossary

53 **modesty** virtue; virginity
54 **dower** dowry
58 **precepts** instructions
63 **flesh-fly** fly that lays eggs in dead flesh
63 **blow** contaminate
71 **boded** intended
81 **Hence, bashful cunning** away with seeming modesty

I am skilless of; but by my modesty,
The jewel in my dower, I would not wish
Any companion in the world but you.   55
Nor can imagination form a shape
Besides yourself to like of. But I prattle
Something too wildly, and my father's precepts
I therein do forget.

Ferdinand   I am in my condition
A prince, Miranda. I do think, a king –   60
I would not so – and would no more endure
This wooden slavery than to suffer
The flesh-fly blow my mouth. Hear my soul speak.
The very instant that I saw you, did
My heart fly to your service, there resides   65
To make me slave to it, and for your sake
Am I this patient log-man.

Miranda   Do you love me?

Ferdinand   O heaven, O earth, bear witness to this sound,
And crown what I profess with kind event
If I speak true. If hollowly, invert   70
What best is boded me to mischief. I,
Beyond all limit of what else i'th'world,
Do love, prize, honour you.

Miranda   I am a fool
To weep at what I am glad of.

Prospero   [Aside] Fair encounter
Of two most rare affections. Heavens rain grace   75
On that which breeds between 'em.

Ferdinand   Wherefore weep you?

Miranda   At mine unworthiness, that dare not offer
What I desire to give, and much less take
What I shall die to want. But this is trifling,
And all the more it seeks to hide itself   80
The bigger bulk it shows. Hence, bashful cunning,

Miranda proposes marriage and Ferdinand willingly agrees. Miranda promises to return soon. Prospero is pleased that this part of his plan is working and goes to bring the other parts of his plan together.

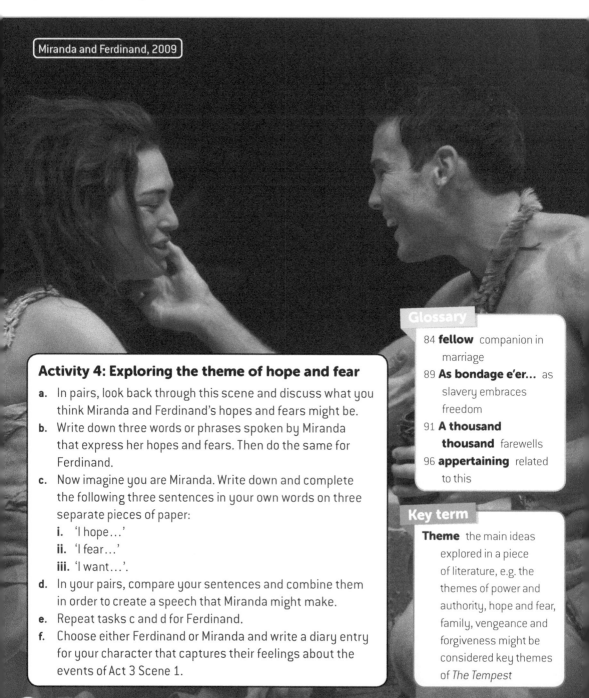

Miranda and Ferdinand, 2009

Activity 4: Exploring the theme of hope and fear

a. In pairs, look back through this scene and discuss what you think Miranda and Ferdinand's hopes and fears might be.
b. Write down three words or phrases spoken by Miranda that express her hopes and fears. Then do the same for Ferdinand.
c. Now imagine you are Miranda. Write down and complete the following three sentences in your own words on three separate pieces of paper:
   i. 'I hope…'
   ii. 'I fear…'
   iii. 'I want…'.
d. In your pairs, compare your sentences and combine them in order to create a speech that Miranda might make.
e. Repeat tasks c and d for Ferdinand.
f. Choose either Ferdinand or Miranda and write a diary entry for your character that captures their feelings about the events of Act 3 Scene 1.

Glossary

84 **fellow** companion in marriage
89 **As bondage e'er…** as slavery embraces freedom
91 **A thousand thousand** farewells
96 **appertaining** related to this

Key term

Theme the main ideas explored in a piece of literature, e.g. the themes of power and authority, hope and fear, family, vengeance and forgiveness might be considered key themes of *The Tempest*

And prompt me, plain and holy innocence.
I am your wife, if you will marry me.
If not, I'll die your maid. To be your fellow
You may deny me, but I'll be your servant   85
Whether you will or no.

Ferdinand   My mistress, dearest,
And I thus humble ever.

Miranda   My husband, then?

Ferdinand   Ay, with a heart as willing
As bondage e'er of freedom. Here's my hand.

Miranda   And mine, with my heart in't. And now farewell   90
Till half an hour hence.

Ferdinand   A thousand thousand.

Exeunt Miranda and Ferdinand separately

Prospero   So glad of this as they I cannot be,
Who are surprised withal; but my rejoicing
At nothing can be more. I'll to my book,
For yet ere supper-time must I perform   95
Much business appertaining.

Exit

Stephano is still taking drunken delight in having Caliban as his servant. Trinculo makes fun of them both.

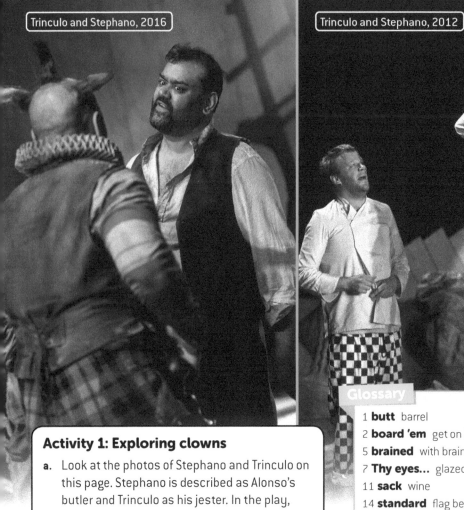

Trinculo and Stephano, 2016

Trinculo and Stephano, 2012

Activity 1: Exploring clowns

a. Look at the photos of Stephano and Trinculo on this page. Stephano is described as Alonso's butler and Trinculo as his jester. In the play, both perform the role of **clowns** to make the audience laugh. How has the designer tried to show their roles through their costumes?

b. Discuss which costume you think works best. Write a paragraph explaining your views.

Glossary

1 **butt** barrel
2 **board 'em** get on board
5 **brained** with brains
7 **Thy eyes...** glazed with drink
11 **sack** wine
14 **standard** flag bearer, with a pun on being able to stand
22 **in case to jostle** ready to jostle
23 **deboshed** debauched; corrupted

At the time

Using page 187, find out more about a king's household in Shakespeare's time to help you understand more about who Trinculo and Stephano are.

Key term

Clown an actor skilled in comedy and improvisation who could often sing and dance as well

Enter Caliban, Stephano and Trinculo

Stephano	Tell not me. When the butt is out we will drink water, not a drop before; therefore bear up, and board 'em. Servant-monster, drink to me.
Trinculo	Servant-monster? The folly of this island. They say there's but five upon this isle. We are three of them. If the other two be brained like us, the state totters.
Stephano	Drink, servant-monster, when I bid thee. Thy eyes are almost set in thy head.
Trinculo	Where should they be set else? He were a brave monster indeed, if they were set in his tail.
Stephano	My man-monster hath drowned his tongue in sack. For my part, the sea cannot drown me. I swam, ere I could recover the shore, five and thirty leagues off and on. By this light, thou shalt be my lieutenant, monster, or my standard.
Trinculo	Your lieutenant, if you list; he's no standard.
Stephano	We'll not run, Monsieur Monster.
Trinculo	Nor go neither; but you'll lie like dogs and yet say nothing neither.
Stephano	Moon-calf, speak once in thy life, if thou beest a good moon-calf.
Caliban	How does thy honour? Let me lick thy shoe. I'll not serve him. He is not valiant.
Trinculo	Thou liest, most ignorant monster. I am in case to jostle a constable. Why, thou deboshed fish thou, was there ever man a coward that hath drunk so much sack as I today? Wilt thou tell a monstrous lie, being but half a fish and half a monster?

5

10

15

20

25

Caliban reminds Stephano of his plea that they defeat Prospero. Stephano makes Trinculo listen to Caliban's plan. Ariel interrupts to call Caliban a liar but, because he is invisible, Caliban and Stephano believe it is Trinculo speaking.

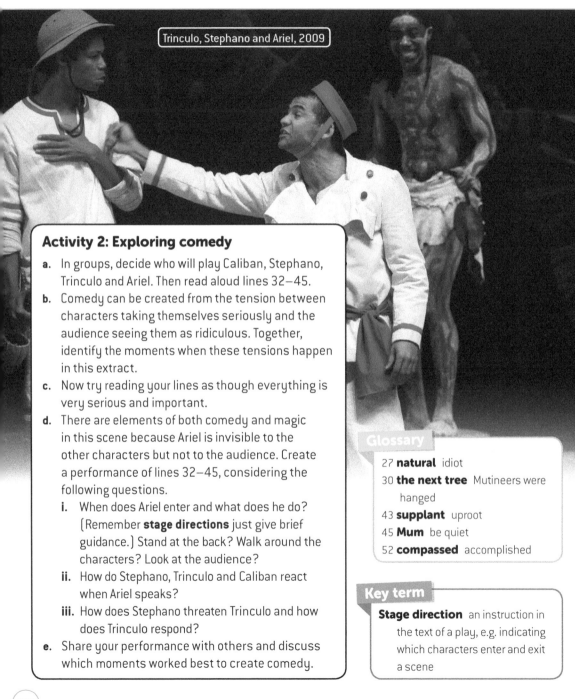

Trinculo, Stephano and Ariel, 2009

Activity 2: Exploring comedy

a. In groups, decide who will play Caliban, Stephano, Trinculo and Ariel. Then read aloud lines 32–45.

b. Comedy can be created from the tension between characters taking themselves seriously and the audience seeing them as ridiculous. Together, identify the moments when these tensions happen in this extract.

c. Now try reading your lines as though everything is very serious and important.

d. There are elements of both comedy and magic in this scene because Ariel is invisible to the other characters but not to the audience. Create a performance of lines 32–45, considering the following questions.

   i. When does Ariel enter and what does he do? (Remember **stage directions** just give brief guidance.) Stand at the back? Walk around the characters? Look at the audience?

   ii. How do Stephano, Trinculo and Caliban react when Ariel speaks?

   iii. How does Stephano threaten Trinculo and how does Trinculo respond?

e. Share your performance with others and discuss which moments worked best to create comedy.

Glossary

27 **natural** idiot
30 **the next tree** Mutineers were hanged
43 **supplant** uproot
45 **Mum** be quiet
52 **compassed** accomplished

Key term

Stage direction an instruction in the text of a play, e.g. indicating which characters enter and exit a scene

Caliban	Lo, how he mocks me! Wilt thou let him, my lord?
Trinculo	'Lord', quoth he. That a monster should be such a natural.
Caliban	Lo, lo, again. Bite him to death, I prithee.
Stephano	Trinculo, keep a good tongue in your head. If you prove a mutineer, the next tree. The poor monster's my subject and he shall not suffer indignity.
Caliban	I thank my noble lord. Wilt thou be pleased To hearken once again to the suit I made to thee?
Stephano	Marry, will I. Kneel and repeat it. I will stand, and so shall Trinculo.

Enter Ariel, invisible

Caliban	As I told thee before, I am subject to a tyrant, a sorcerer, that by his cunning hath cheated me of the island.
Ariel	Thou liest.
Caliban	[To Trinculo] Thou liest, thou jesting monkey, thou. I would my valiant master would destroy thee. I do not lie.
Stephano	Trinculo, if you trouble him any more in's tale, by this hand, I will supplant some of your teeth.
Trinculo	Why, I said nothing.
Stephano	Mum then, and no more. [To Caliban] Proceed.
Caliban	I say by sorcery he got this isle; From me he got it. If thy greatness will Revenge it on him – for I know thou dar'st, But this thing dare not—
Stephano	That's most certain.
Caliban	Thou shalt be lord of it, and I'll serve thee.
Stephano	How now shall this be compassed? Canst thou bring me to the party?

30

35

40

45

50

111

Caliban describes his plan that Stephano should kill Prospero while he is sleeping. Ariel continues to interrupt, accusing Caliban and then Stephano of lying. They continue to believe it is Trinculo speaking.

Stephano, Ariel and Caliban, 2006

Activity 3: Exploring Caliban's plan

a. In pairs, together read aloud Caliban's speech in lines 78–85.

b. List all the action **verbs** in this speech and speak them aloud. What feelings do these words suggest when you speak them?

c. Find gestures for each of these verbs and for any other words or phrases in this speech you want to emphasise.

d. Read aloud the speech again, adding in the gestures.

e. Discuss why you think Caliban has not tried to kill Prospero himself.

f. Choose three words of your own to describe how Caliban feels about Prospero.

g. Look at the photo on this page. Which line do you think is being spoken at this moment?

Glossary

57 **pied ninny... scurvy patch** references to Trinculo's role as a jester. Jesters wore multi-coloured costumes

61 **quick freshes** freshwater streams

64 **stockfish** dried fish

71 **murrain** plague

81 **paunch** stab in the stomach

82 **weasand** windpipe

84 **sot** fool, drunkard

Key term

Verb a word describing an action or a state, e.g. *jump, shout, believe, exist*

Caliban	Yea, yea, my lord. I'll yield him thee asleep,
	Where thou mayst knock a nail into his head.

55

Ariel	Thou liest, thou canst not.

Caliban	What a pied ninny's this? [To Trinculo] Thou scurvy patch!
	[To Stephano] I do beseech thy greatness give him blows,
	And take his bottle from him. When that's gone
	He shall drink nought but brine, for I'll not show him
	Where the quick freshes are.

60

Stephano	Trinculo, run into no further danger. Interrupt the monster one
	word further, and by this hand, I'll turn my mercy out o'doors and
	make a stockfish of thee.

Trinculo	Why, what did I? I did nothing. I'll go farther off.

65

Stephano	Didst thou not say he lied?

Ariel	Thou liest.

Stephano	Do I so? [Strikes Trinculo] Take thou that. As you like this, give me
	the lie another time.

Trinculo	I did not give the lie. Out o'your wits and hearing too? A pox
	o'your bottle! This can sack and drinking do. A murrain on your
	monster, and the devil take your fingers!

70

Caliban	Ha, ha, ha!

Stephano	Now, forward with your tale. [To Trinculo] Prithee, stand farther off.

Caliban	Beat him enough. After a little time,
	I'll beat him too.

75

Stephano	[To Trinculo] Stand farther. [To Caliban] Come, proceed.

Caliban	Why, as I told thee, 'tis a custom with him
	I'th'afternoon to sleep. There thou mayst brain him,
	Having first seized his books; or with a log
	Batter his skull, or paunch him with a stake,
	Or cut his weasand with thy knife. Remember
	First to possess his books, for without them
	He's but a sot, as I am, nor hath not

80

Caliban tells Stephano that after murdering Prospero he should burn all his books and take the beautiful Miranda as his wife. Stephano agrees to the plan and makes friends again with Trinculo. They begin to sing.

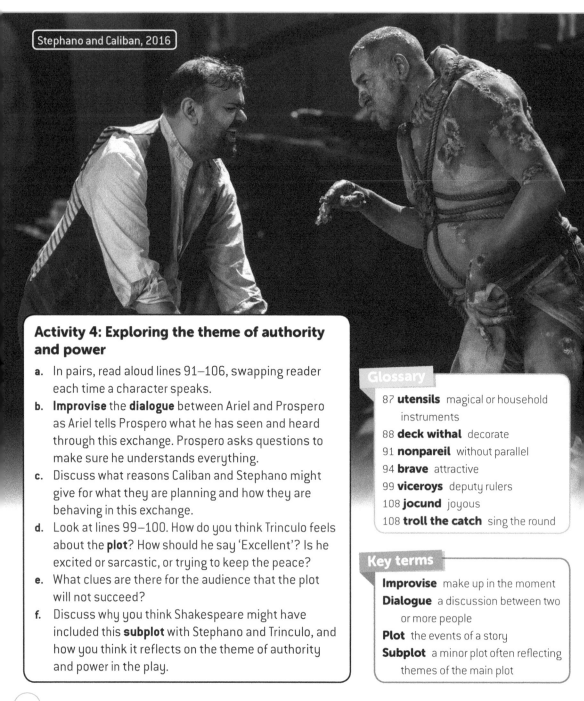

Stephano and Caliban, 2016

Activity 4: Exploring the theme of authority and power

a. In pairs, read aloud lines 91–106, swapping reader each time a character speaks.

b. **Improvise** the **dialogue** between Ariel and Prospero as Ariel tells Prospero what he has seen and heard through this exchange. Prospero asks questions to make sure he understands everything.

c. Discuss what reasons Caliban and Stephano might give for what they are planning and how they are behaving in this exchange.

d. Look at lines 99–100. How do you think Trinculo feels about the **plot**? How should he say 'Excellent'? Is he excited or sarcastic, or trying to keep the peace?

e. What clues are there for the audience that the plot will not succeed?

f. Discuss why you think Shakespeare might have included this **subplot** with Stephano and Trinculo, and how you think it reflects on the theme of authority and power in the play.

Glossary

87 **utensils** magical or household instruments
88 **deck withal** decorate
91 **nonpareil** without parallel
94 **brave** attractive
99 **viceroys** deputy rulers
108 **jocund** joyous
108 **troll the catch** sing the round

Key terms

Improvise make up in the moment
Dialogue a discussion between two or more people
Plot the events of a story
Subplot a minor plot often reflecting themes of the main plot

	One spirit to command. They all do hate him	85
	As rootedly as I. Burn but his books.	
	He has brave utensils, for so he calls them,	
	Which when he has a house, he'll deck withal.	
	And that most deeply to consider is	
	The beauty of his daughter. He himself	90
	Calls her a nonpareil. I never saw a woman,	
	But only Sycorax my dam, and she;	
	But she as far surpasseth Sycorax	
	As great'st does least.	

| Stephano | Is it so brave a lass? | |

| Caliban | Ay, lord. She will become thy bed, I warrant, | 95 |
| | And bring thee forth brave brood. | |

| Stephano | Monster, I will kill this man. His daughter and I will be king and queen – save our graces! – and Trinculo and thyself shall be viceroys. Dost thou like the plot, Trinculo? | |

| Trinculo | Excellent. | 100 |

| Stephano | Give me thy hand, I am sorry I beat thee. But, while thou livest, keep a good tongue in thy head. | |

| Caliban | Within this half hour will he be asleep. Wilt thou destroy him then? | |

| Stephano | Ay, on mine honour. | 105 |

| Ariel | [Aside] This will I tell my master. | |

| Caliban | Thou mak'st me merry. I am full of pleasure, Let us be jocund. Will you troll the catch You taught me but while-ere? | |

| Stephano | At thy request, monster, I will do reason, any reason. Come on, Trinculo, let us sing. [Sings] Flout 'em and scout 'em And scout 'em and flout 'em, Thought is free. | 110 |

| Caliban | That's not the tune. | 115 |

Ariel plays a tune similar to the song Stephano and Trinculo are singing. Caliban tells them not to be scared because the island is full of beautiful music. They decide to follow the music before they kill Prospero.

Activity 5: Exploring Caliban's language

a. In groups, read aloud lines 124–132, swapping reader at each punctuation mark.
b. One of you read aloud the speech again, while the others listen and repeat any words they like the sound of.
c. Agree gestures for the key words in the speech and create a performance of this speech, adding in the gestures and considering tone, emphasis, pace, volume and repetition.
d. Look back at Caliban's speech in lines 78–88 and discuss the differences between that speech and this one.
e. Create two **statues**: one showing how Caliban might appear as he speaks the first speech and the second how he might appear as he speaks the second speech.
f. Discuss why you think Shakespeare includes this second speech at this moment. What does it suggest about Caliban?
g. Write a paragraph or two predicting what you think will happen next in this subplot of Caliban, Stephano and Trinculo. Give reasons for your predictions.

Glossary

117 **Nobody** someone invisible
119 **list** wish
138 **taborer** drummer, playing the strange music

Key terms

Statue like a **freeze-frame** but often of a single character, and can be more abstract
Freeze-frame a physical, still image created by people to represent an object, place, person or feeling

Stephano, Caliban and Trinculo, 2006

Ariel plays the tune on a tabor and pipe

Stephano	What is this same?
Trinculo	This is the tune of our catch, played by the picture of Nobody.
Stephano	If thou beest a man, show thyself in thy likeness. If thou beest a devil, take it as thou list.
Trinculo	O, forgive me my sins.
Stephano	He that dies pays all debts. I defy thee. Mercy upon us.
Caliban	Art thou afeard?
Stephano	No, monster, not I.
Caliban	Be not afeard, the isle is full of noises,

Stephano What is this same?

Trinculo This is the tune of our catch, played by the picture of Nobody.

Stephano If thou beest a man, show thyself in thy likeness. If thou beest a
devil, take it as thou list.

Trinculo O, forgive me my sins. 120

Stephano He that dies pays all debts. I defy thee. Mercy upon us.

Caliban Art thou afeard?

Stephano No, monster, not I.

Caliban Be not afeard, the isle is full of noises,
Sounds and sweet airs, that give delight and hurt not. 125
Sometimes a thousand twangling instruments
Will hum about mine ears; and sometime voices,
That if I then had waked after long sleep,
Will make me sleep again, and then in dreaming,
The clouds methought would open and show riches 130
Ready to drop upon me, that when I waked
I cried to dream again.

Stephano This will prove a brave kingdom to me, where I shall have my
music for nothing.

Caliban When Prospero is destroyed. 135

Stephano That shall be by and by. I remember the story.

Trinculo The sound is going away. Let's follow it, and after do our work.

Stephano Lead, monster, we'll follow. I would I could see this taborer; he lays
it on.

Trinculo [To Caliban] Wilt come? I'll follow Stephano. 140

Exeunt

Gonzalo complains that he needs to rest and Alonso agrees. Antonio reminds Sebastian of the plan to murder Gonzalo and Alonso, and they agree to do it that night. The spirits of the island appear with music and lay out a banquet.

Sebastian and Antonio, 2012

Glossary

1 **By'r lakin** by our ladykin, the Virgin Mary
2 **maze** network of tracks
3 **Through forth-rights...** straight and winding paths
12 **repulse** setback
12 **forgo** give up
13 **advantage** opportunity
15 **travail** labour; travelling

Activity 1: Exploring staging

a. In groups, read aloud lines 1–17, swapping reader at the end of each sentence.
b. Together, agree a paraphrase of each speech.
c. Create a freeze-frame of this moment, which makes clear the characters' attitudes to their situation and to each other. Look at the photo on this page to help you, adding in other characters.
d. Look at the stage direction in the middle of line 17 and discuss how you might bring this action to life. How will your spirits move and sound?
e. Decide who will play Gonzalo, Alonso, Sebastian, Antonio and the spirits, including other characters as best suits your group. Create a performance of lines 1–19, which uses the ideas and understanding you have shared from tasks a–c.

Key term

Staging the process of selecting, adapting and developing the stage space in which a play will be performed

Enter Alonso, Sebastian, Antonio, Gonzalo, Adrian, Francisco and others

Gonzalo By'r lakin, I can go no further, sir,
My old bones ache. Here's a maze trod indeed
Through forth-rights and meanders. By your patience,
I needs must rest me.

Alonso   Old lord, I cannot blame thee,
Who am myself attached with weariness   5
To th'dulling of my spirits. Sit down and rest.
Even here I will put off my hope, and keep it
No longer for my flatterer. He is drowned
Whom thus we stray to find, and the sea mocks
Our frustrate search on land. Well, let him go.   10

Antonio [Aside to Sebastian] I am right glad that he's so out of hope.
Do not for one repulse forgo the purpose
That you resolved t'effect.

Sebastian   [Aside to Antonio] The next advantage
Will we take thoroughly.

Antonio   [Aside to Sebastian] Let it be tonight.
For now they are oppressed with travail, they   15
Will not, nor cannot use such vigilance
As when they are fresh.

Solemn and strange music. Enter Prospero on the top, invisible.
Enter several strange shapes, bringing in a banquet, and dance
about it with gentle actions of salutations, and inviting the King, etc.
to eat, they depart

Sebastian   [Aside to Antonio] I say tonight. No more.

Alonso What harmony is this? My good friends, hark.

Gonzalo Marvellous sweet music.

The nobles discuss the strangeness of the creatures they see. The spirits disappear when they have laid out the banquet and the nobles discuss whether they should eat.

Activity 2: Exploring Prospero's point of view

a. In groups, read aloud Gonzalo's lines 27–34 and Prospero's response in lines 34–36.

b. Decide who will play Prospero and then create a freeze-frame of this moment with Alonso, Gonzalo, Sebastian and Antonio.

c. 'Prospero' should then alter the freeze-frame, making each character appear how he sees them. For example, he might see Gonzalo as very upright and open, while he might see Antonio as hunched over, rubbing his hands as he plots about others.

d. Decide how Prospero would describe each character in one line of modern English.

e. 'Prospero' then speaks each line of description, which cues that character into 2–3 seconds of action reflecting that description.

Glossary

21 **drollery** comic play; puppet show

25 **want credit** lack credibility

30 **certes** certainly

33 **generation** race

41 **viands** food

44 **mountaineers** people who live in the mountains

Antonio, Spirit, Gonzalo, Spirit and Sebastian, 2016

Alonso	Give us kind keepers, heavens. What were these? 20
Sebastian	A living drollery. Now I will believe
	That there are unicorns; that in Arabia
	There is one tree, the phoenix' throne, one phoenix
	At this hour reigning there.
Antonio	I'll believe both.
	And what does else want credit, come to me, 25
	And I'll be sworn 'tis true. Travellers ne'er did lie,
	Though fools at home condemn 'em.
Gonzalo	If in Naples
	I should report this now, would they believe me?
	If I should say I saw such islanders,
	For certes these are people of the island, 30
	Who though they are of monstrous shape, yet note
	Their manners are more gentle, kind, than of
	Our human generation you shall find
	Many, nay almost any.
Prospero	[Aside] Honest lord,
	Thou hast said well; for some of you there present 35
	Are worse than devils.
Alonso	I cannot too much muse
	Such shapes, such gesture, and such sound, expressing,
	Although they want the use of tongue, a kind
	Of excellent dumb discourse.
Prospero	[Aside] Praise in departing.
Francisco	They vanished strangely.
Sebastian	No matter, since 40
	They have left their viands behind; for we have stomachs.
	Will't please you taste of what is here?
Alonso	Not I.
Gonzalo	Faith, sir, you need not fear. When we were boys,
	Who would believe that there were mountaineers,

Ariel suddenly appears as a harpy and casts a spell, sending Alonso, Sebastian and Antonio into madness. He declares that he is acting as an agent of Fate, bringing the nobles the punishment they deserve for their treatment of Prospero.

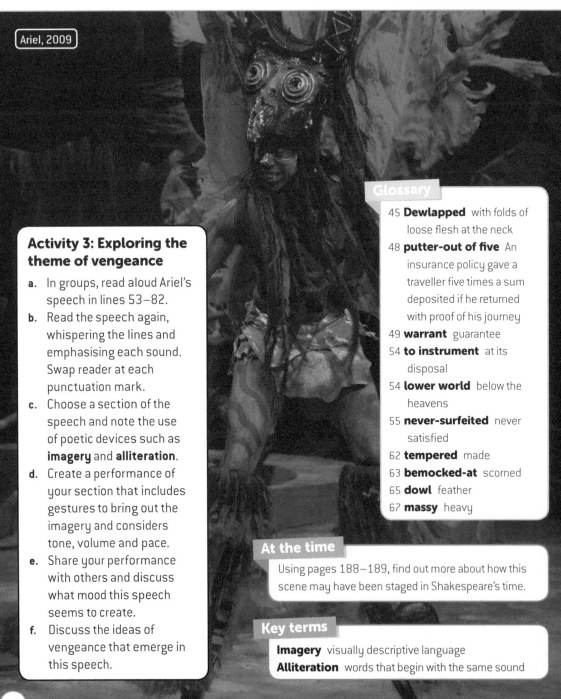

Ariel, 2009

Activity 3: Exploring the theme of vengeance

a. In groups, read aloud Ariel's speech in lines 53–82.

b. Read the speech again, whispering the lines and emphasising each sound. Swap reader at each punctuation mark.

c. Choose a section of the speech and note the use of poetic devices such as **imagery** and **alliteration**.

d. Create a performance of your section that includes gestures to bring out the imagery and considers tone, volume and pace.

e. Share your performance with others and discuss what mood this speech seems to create.

f. Discuss the ideas of vengeance that emerge in this speech.

Glossary

45 **Dewlapped** with folds of loose flesh at the neck
48 **putter-out of five** An insurance policy gave a traveller five times a sum deposited if he returned with proof of his journey
49 **warrant** guarantee
54 **to instrument** at its disposal
54 **lower world** below the heavens
55 **never-surfeited** never satisfied
62 **tempered** made
63 **bemocked-at** scorned
65 **dowl** feather
67 **massy** heavy

At the time

Using pages 188–189, find out more about how this scene may have been staged in Shakespeare's time.

Key terms

Imagery visually descriptive language
Alliteration words that begin with the same sound

Dewlapped like bulls, whose throats had hanging at 'em   45
Wallets of flesh? Or that there were such men
Whose heads stood in their breasts? Which now we find
Each putter-out of five for one will bring us
Good warrant of.

Alonso   I will stand to, and feed,
Although my last, no matter, since I feel   50
The best is past. Brother, my lord the duke,
Stand to, and do as we.

Thunder and lightning. Enter Ariel, like a harpy, claps his wings upon the
table, and with a quaint device, the banquet vanishes

Ariel   You are three men of sin, whom destiny,
That hath to instrument this lower world
And what is in't, the never-surfeited sea,   55
Hath caused to belch up you; and on this island,
Where man doth not inhabit, you 'mongst men
Being most unfit to live. I have made you mad;
And even with such-like valour men hang and drown
Their proper selves.

Alonso, Sebastian and Antonio draw their swords

                    You fools. I and my fellows   60
Are ministers of Fate. The elements
Of whom your swords are tempered may as well
Wound the loud winds, or with bemocked-at stabs
Kill the still-closing waters, as diminish
One dowl that's in my plume. My fellow ministers   65
Are like invulnerable. If you could hurt,
Your swords are now too massy for your strengths,
And will not be uplifted. But remember,
For that's my business to you, that you three
From Milan did supplant good Prospero;   70
Exposed unto the sea, which hath requit it,
Him and his innocent child. For which foul deed,
The powers, delaying, not forgetting, have
Incensed the seas and shores, yea, all the creatures

Prospero praises Ariel's performance and notes that his plans have all come together. Alonso is convinced his behaviour towards Prospero has resulted in the death of Ferdinand and sets off to drown himself.

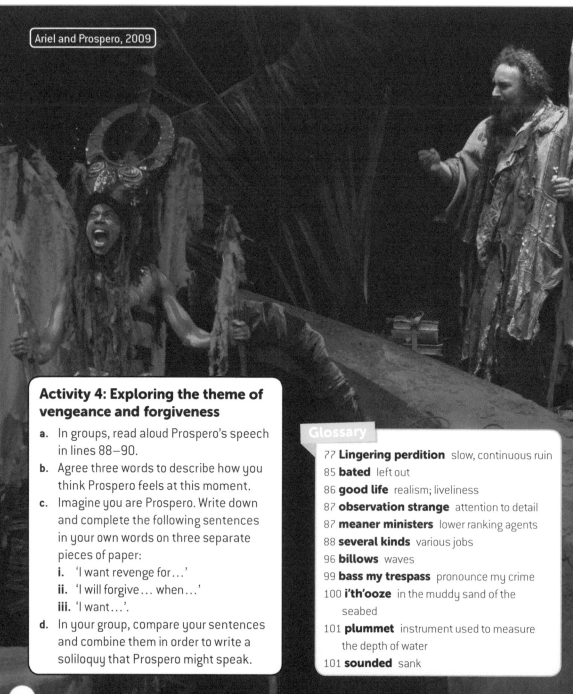

Ariel and Prospero, 2009

Activity 4: Exploring the theme of vengeance and forgiveness

a. In groups, read aloud Prospero's speech in lines 88–90.

b. Agree three words to describe how you think Prospero feels at this moment.

c. Imagine you are Prospero. Write down and complete the following sentences in your own words on three separate pieces of paper:
   i. 'I want revenge for…'
   ii. 'I will forgive… when…'
   iii. 'I want…'.

d. In your group, compare your sentences and combine them in order to write a soliloquy that Prospero might speak.

Glossary

77 Lingering perdition slow, continuous ruin

85 bated left out

86 good life realism; liveliness

87 observation strange attention to detail

87 meaner ministers lower ranking agents

88 several kinds various jobs

96 billows waves

99 bass my trespass pronounce my crime

100 i'th'ooze in the muddy sand of the seabed

101 plummet instrument used to measure the depth of water

101 sounded sank

Against your peace. Thee of thy son, Alonso, 75
They have bereft; and do pronounce by me
Lingering perdition, worse than any death
Can be at once, shall step by step attend
You and your ways; whose wraths to guard you from,
Which here in this most desolate isle else falls 80
Upon your heads, is nothing but heart's sorrow
And a clear life ensuing.

Ariel vanishes in thunder. Then, to soft music, enter the shapes again, and
dance, with mocks and mows, and carrying out the table. They depart

Prospero Bravely the figure of this harpy hast thou
Performed, my Ariel; a grace it had, devouring.
Of my instruction hast thou nothing bated 85
In what thou hadst to say. So, with good life
And observation strange, my meaner ministers
Their several kinds have done. My high charms work,
And these, mine enemies, are all knit up
In their distractions. They now are in my power, 90
And in these fits I leave them, while I visit
Young Ferdinand, whom they suppose is drowned,
And his and mine loved darling.

Exit Prospero

Gonzalo I'th'name of something holy, sir, why stand you
In this strange stare?

Alonso   O, it is monstrous, monstrous. 95
Methought the billows spoke and told me of it,
The winds did sing it to me, and the thunder,
That deep and dreadful organ-pipe, pronounced
The name of Prosper. It did bass my trespass.
Therefore my son i'th'ooze is bedded; and 100
I'll seek him deeper than e'er plummet sounded
And with him there lie mudded.

Exit Alonso

Sebastian   But one fiend at a time,
I'll fight their legions o'er.

Gonzalo tells Adrian and Francisco to chase after Alonso, Sebastian and Antonio because their guilt seems to have sent them into madness and they might cause themselves harm.

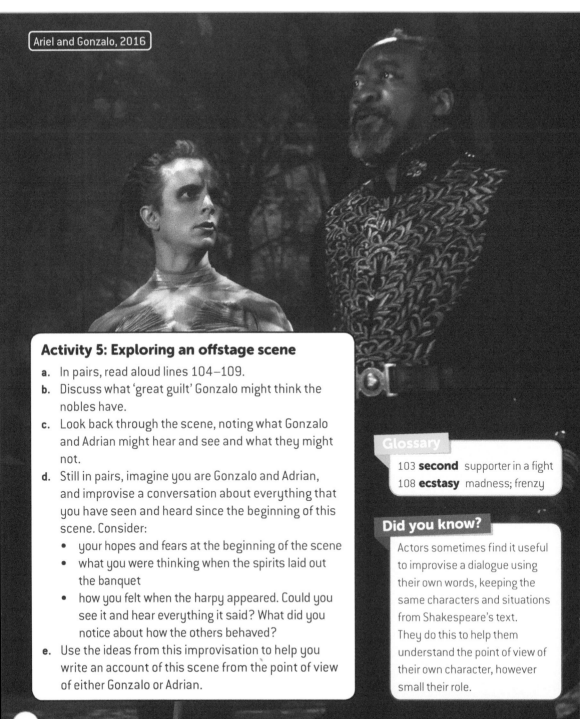

Ariel and Gonzalo, 2016

Activity 5: Exploring an offstage scene

a. In pairs, read aloud lines 104–109.
b. Discuss what 'great guilt' Gonzalo might think the nobles have.
c. Look back through the scene, noting what Gonzalo and Adrian might hear and see and what they might not.
d. Still in pairs, imagine you are Gonzalo and Adrian, and improvise a conversation about everything that you have seen and heard since the beginning of this scene. Consider:
   - your hopes and fears at the beginning of the scene
   - what you were thinking when the spirits laid out the banquet
   - how you felt when the harpy appeared. Could you see it and hear everything it said? What did you notice about how the others behaved?
e. Use the ideas from this improvisation to help you write an account of this scene from the point of view of either Gonzalo or Adrian.

Glossary

103 **second** supporter in a fight
108 **ecstasy** madness; frenzy

Did you know?

Actors sometimes find it useful to improvise a dialogue using their own words, keeping the same characters and situations from Shakespeare's text. They do this to help them understand the point of view of their own character, however small their role.

Antonio   I'll be thy second.

Gonzalo All three of them are desperate. Their great guilt,
Like poison given to work a great time after,   105
Now 'gins to bite the spirits. I do beseech you,
That are of suppler joints, follow them swiftly
And hinder them from what this ecstasy
May now provoke them to.

Adrian   Follow, I pray you.

Exploring Act 3

Sebastian, Ariel,
Gonzalo, Adrian, Alonso
and Francisco, 2012

Activity 1: Exploring points of view

a. In groups, choose one of the three scenes in Act 3
and remind yourselves what happens in it.

b. Which of the following themes do you feel is most
powerfully presented in your scene and why?
- Authority and power
- Hope and fear
- Family
- Vengeance and forgiveness

c. Each person in your group chooses a different
character appearing in your scene. Each person
writes a **monologue** in modern English in which
their character retells the events of the scene
from their point of view and how they feel about
what happened.

d. Add a sentence from your own point of view about
which theme you think most underpins your
character's thoughts and actions, and why.

e. Add a further sentence, which predicts what you
think will happen to your character in the next Act.

Key term

Monologue a long speech in
which a character expresses
their thoughts. Other
characters may be present

Activity 2: Designing the island

The action of the play takes place on, or just off the coast of, an island. A director and designer have to consider what impression of the island they want to give the audience and how to show changes of place and mood for each scene. Imagine you are creating a design for a production of *The Tempest*. Make notes in response to the following points.

i.   How specific do you want to be about climate, flora and fauna? The design of the RSC production in 2006 showed an island in the Arctic Circle, while the production in 2009 showed an African island. Other productions have been more abstract.

ii. Will your set be linked to the shipwreck? Some designs suggest wrecked ships or items that have been washed ashore, as in the RSC productions in 2012 and 2016.

iii. Look back over Act 3. Use the page summaries to help you remember what happens. How would you describe the overall mood of each scene? How might it feel for each group of characters to be on the magical island? Exciting? Scary? Beautiful? What colours might suit that mood?

iv. How will you show the key elements for each scene: the logs in Scene 1; the presence of Ariel (unseen by the other characters) in Scene 2; and Ariel's harpy in Scene 3?

Write a detailed description, draw or make a model of your stage design for Act 3, which includes the key elements for each scene.

Did you know?

Directors and designers work closely together on the look and feel of a production based on their close reading of the text. The designer creates a model box of the set, and photos and drawings might be stuck up on the walls of the rehearsal room to give the company a sense of the design ideas.

Prospero tells Ferdinand how valuable Miranda is and warns him not to sleep with her before they are properly married. Ferdinand says he would not think of it.

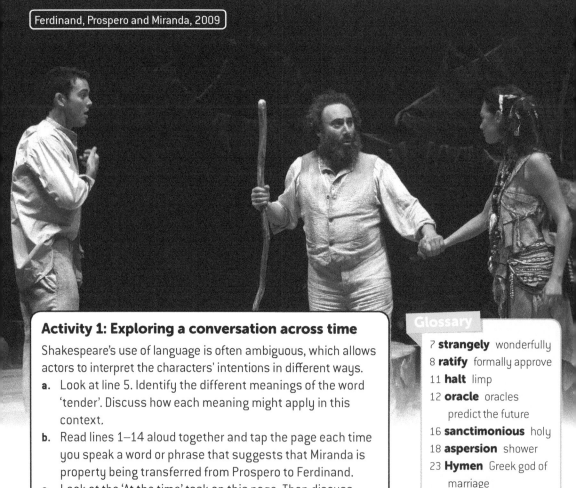

Ferdinand, Prospero and Miranda, 2009

Activity 1: Exploring a conversation across time

Shakespeare's use of language is often ambiguous, which allows actors to interpret the characters' intentions in different ways.

a. Look at line 5. Identify the different meanings of the word 'tender'. Discuss how each meaning might apply in this context.

b. Read lines 1–14 aloud together and tap the page each time you speak a word or phrase that suggests that Miranda is property being transferred from Prospero to Ferdinand.

c. Look at the 'At the time' task on this page. Then discuss how an audience in Shakespeare's time might respond to the words and phrases you identified in task b and how an audience today might respond.

d. Read the lines again, swapping reader at the end of each sentence. Read through once as if this is a business transaction between the two men and the second time as if Prospero is very reluctant to lose his daughter.

e. Which version do you think is closer to how the production shown in the photo on this page interpreted Prospero's attitude?

Glossary

7 **strangely** wonderfully
8 **ratify** formally approve
11 **halt** limp
12 **oracle** oracles predict the future
16 **sanctimonious** holy
18 **aspersion** shower
23 **Hymen** Greek god of marriage
24 **issue** children

At the time

Using pages 194–195, find out more about marriage and courtship in Shakespeare's time to help you with the activity on this page.

Act 4 | Scene 1

Enter Prospero, Ferdinand and Miranda

Prospero [To Ferdinand] If I have too austerely punished you,
Your compensation makes amends, for I
Have given you here a third of mine own life,
Or that for which I live, who once again
I tender to thy hand. All thy vexations   5
Were but my trials of thy love, and thou
Hast strangely stood the test. Here, afore heaven,
I ratify this my rich gift. O Ferdinand,
Do not smile at me that I boast her of,
For thou shalt find she will outstrip all praise   10
And make it halt behind her.

Ferdinand   I do believe it
Against an oracle.

Prospero Then, as my gift, and thine own acquisition
Worthily purchased, take my daughter. But
If thou dost break her virgin-knot before   15
All sanctimonious ceremonies may
With full and holy rite be ministered,
No sweet aspersion shall the heavens let fall
To make this contract grow; but barren hate,
Sour-eyed disdain and discord shall bestrew   20
The union of your bed, with weeds so loathly
That you shall hate it both. Therefore take heed,
As Hymen's lamps shall light you.

Ferdinand   As I hope
For quiet days, fair issue and long life,
With such love as 'tis now, the murkiest den,   25
The most opportune place, the strongest suggestion
Our worser genius can, shall never melt
Mine honour into lust, to take away

Prospero calls Ariel and tells him to bring the spirits of the island to create a show to celebrate Miranda and Ferdinand's betrothal.

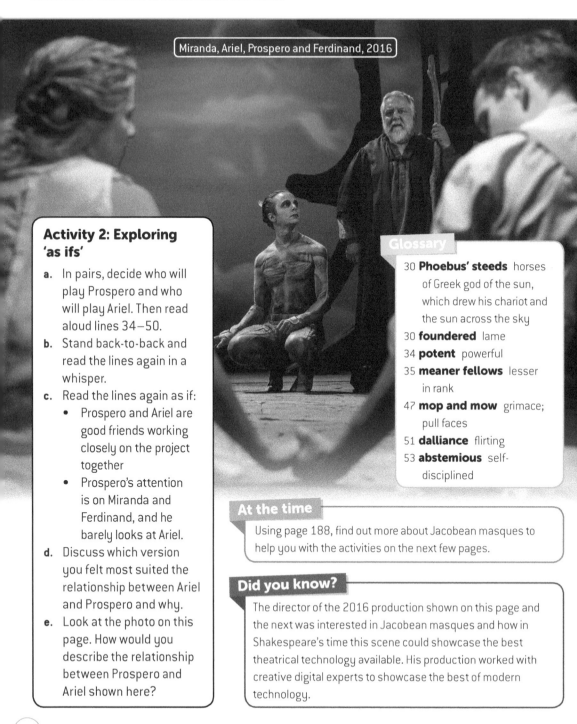

Miranda, Ariel, Prospero and Ferdinand, 2016

Activity 2: Exploring 'as ifs'

a. In pairs, decide who will play Prospero and who will play Ariel. Then read aloud lines 34–50.

b. Stand back-to-back and read the lines again in a whisper.

c. Read the lines again as if:
   - Prospero and Ariel are good friends working closely on the project together
   - Prospero's attention is on Miranda and Ferdinand, and he barely looks at Ariel.

d. Discuss which version you felt most suited the relationship between Ariel and Prospero and why.

e. Look at the photo on this page. How would you describe the relationship between Prospero and Ariel shown here?

Glossary

30 **Phoebus' steeds** horses of Greek god of the sun, which drew his chariot and the sun across the sky

30 **foundered** lame

34 **potent** powerful

35 **meaner fellows** lesser in rank

47 **mop and mow** grimace; pull faces

51 **dalliance** flirting

53 **abstemious** self-disciplined

At the time

Using page 188, find out more about Jacobean masques to help you with the activities on the next few pages.

Did you know?

The director of the 2016 production shown on this page and the next was interested in Jacobean masques and how in Shakespeare's time this scene could showcase the best theatrical technology available. His production worked with creative digital experts to showcase the best of modern technology.

	The edge of that day's celebration
	When I shall think or Phoebus' steeds are foundered,	30
	Or night kept chained below.

Prospero   Fairly spoke.
Sit then and talk with her. She is thine own.
What, Ariel! My industrious servant, Ariel!

Enter Ariel

Ariel   What would my potent master? Here I am.

Prospero   Thou and thy meaner fellows your last service   35
Did worthily perform, and I must use you
In such another trick. Go bring the rabble,
O'er whom I give thee power, here to this place.
Incite them to quick motion, for I must
Bestow upon the eyes of this young couple   40
Some vanity of mine art. It is my promise,
And they expect it from me.

Ariel   Presently?

Prospero   Ay, with a twink.

Ariel   Before you can say 'come' and 'go',
And breathe twice and cry 'so, so',   45
Each one, tripping on his toe,
Will be here with mop and mow.
Do you love me, master? No?

Prospero   Dearly, my delicate Ariel. Do not approach
Till thou dost hear me call.

Ariel   Well, I conceive.   50

Exit Ariel

Prospero   [To Ferdinand] Look thou be true. Do not give dalliance
Too much the rein. The strongest oaths are straw
To the fire i'th'blood. Be more abstemious,
Or else good night your vow.

The spirits' show begins with the appearance of Iris, goddess of the rainbow and messenger to the other gods. Iris calls Ceres, goddess of the harvest. Ceres appears and asks why she has been summoned.

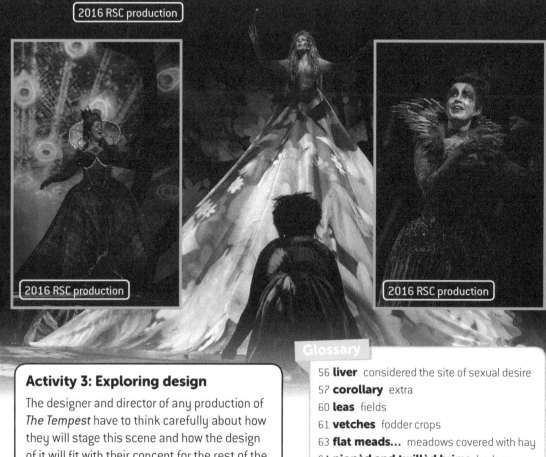

2016 RSC production

2016 RSC production

2016 RSC production

Activity 3: Exploring design

The designer and director of any production of *The Tempest* have to think carefully about how they will stage this scene and how the design of it will fit with their concept for the rest of the production.

a. Look at the photos on this page. Which goddess do you think is being depicted in each photo and what clues from the text help you decide? Discuss which design ideas you think are the most interesting.

b. Look back at lines 39–42 and discuss why you think Prospero promised this show for Miranda and Ferdinand. Write a sentence or two summarising your discussion.

Glossary

56 **liver** considered the site of sexual desire
57 **corollary** extra
60 **leas** fields
61 **vetches** fodder crops
63 **flat meads...** meadows covered with hay
64 **pionèd and twillèd brims** hedges
66 **broom-groves** groves of broom, a yellow-flowered shrub
68 **lass-lorn** missing a girlfriend
68 **poll-clipped** pruned
69 **sea-marge** sea shore
70 **air** take the air
71 **watery arch** rainbow
74 **peacocks** Roman goddess Juno's chariot was drawn by peacocks
74 **amain** swiftly
81 **bosky** bushy

Ferdinand	I warrant you, sir,

    The white cold virgin snow upon my heart   55
    Abates the ardour of my liver.

Prospero   Well.

    Now come, my Ariel! Bring a corollary,
    Rather than want a spirit: appear, and pertly.
    No tongue! All eyes! Be silent!

Soft music. Enter Iris

Iris   Ceres, most bounteous lady, thy rich leas   60
    Of wheat, rye, barley, vetches, oats and peas;
    Thy turfy mountains, where live nibbling sheep,
    And flat meads thatched with stover, them to keep;
    Thy banks with pionèd and twillèd brims,
    Which spongy April at thy hest betrims   65
    To make cold nymphs chaste crowns; and thy broom-groves,
    Whose shadow the dismissèd bachelor loves,
    Being lass-lorn; thy poll-clipped vineyard,
    And thy sea-marge sterile and rocky-hard,
    Where thou thyself dost air: the queen o'th'sky,   70
    Whose watery arch and messenger am I,
    Bids thee leave these, and with her sovereign grace,

Juno descends

    Here on this grass-plot, in this very place,
    To come and sport. Her peacocks fly amain.
    Approach, rich Ceres, her to entertain.   75

Enter Ceres

Ceres   Hail, many-coloured messenger, that ne'er
    Dost disobey the wife of Jupiter;
    Who, with thy saffron wings, upon my flowers
    Diffusest honey drops, refreshing showers,
    And with each end of thy blue bow dost crown   80
    My bosky acres and my unshrubbed down,
    Rich scarf to my proud earth. Why hath thy queen
    Summoned me hither to this short-grassed green?

Iris tells Ceres they are there to bless the betrothal of Miranda and Ferdinand and that Venus and Cupid are not around to tempt the young lovers into sex before marriage. Juno arrives and the goddesses bless the couple.

Activity 4: Exploring language

a. In groups, read lines 106–117, swapping reader at the end of each line.
b. Discuss what you notice about rhythm and rhyme in these lines.
c. Choose one of the **quatrains** and work out a way to present it, considering how you will use **gesture**, **tone**, volume and **emphasis**.
d. Rehearse your performance and then share it with others.

Key terms

Quatrain a stanza of four lines
Gesture a movement, often using the hands or head, to express a feeling or idea
Tone as in 'tone of voice'; expressing an attitude through how you say something
Emphasis stress given to words when speaking

Glossary

85 **estate** bestow
86 **bow** rainbow
87 **Venus or her son** Venus was the Roman goddess of love and her son was Cupid the god of sexual desire
89 **dusky Dis** dark Pluto, Roman god of the underworld. He kidnapped Ceres' daughter Persephone with the help of Venus and Cupid
90 **blind boy** Cupid is often depicted as blindfolded
93 **Paphos** city in Cyprus that worshipped Venus
94 **Dove-drawn** Venus' chariot was drawn by doves
95 **wanton charm** tempt them to lust
96 **bed-right** sex
98 **Mars's hot minion** Venus, who was the lover of Mars, god of war
99 **waspish-headed** someone who stings; spiteful
102 **gait** way of walking
110 **foison** abundance
111 **garners** granaries

Iris	A contract of true love to celebrate,
	And some donation freely to estate 85
	On the blest lovers.
Ceres	Tell me, heavenly bow,
	If Venus or her son, as thou dost know,
	Do now attend the queen? Since they did plot
	The means that dusky Dis my daughter got,
	Her and her blind boy's scandaled company 90
	I have forsworn.
Iris	Of her society
	Be not afraid. I met her deity
	Cutting the clouds towards Paphos, and her son
	Dove-drawn with her. Here thought they to have done
	Some wanton charm upon this man and maid, 95
	Whose vows are that no bed-right shall be paid
	Till Hymen's torch be lighted; but in vain.
	Mars's hot minion is returned again.
	Her waspish-headed son has broke his arrows,
	Swears he will shoot no more, but play with sparrows, 100
	And be a boy right out.
Ceres	Highest queen of state,
	Great Juno, comes; I know her by her gait.
Juno	How does my bounteous sister? Go with me
	To bless this twain, that they may prosperous be,
	And honoured in their issue. 105

They sing

Juno	Honour, riches, marriage-blessing,
	Long continuance, and increasing,
	Hourly joys be still upon you,
	Juno sings her blessings on you.
Ceres	Earth's increase, foison plenty, 110
	Barns and garners never empty,
	Vines with clustering bunches growing,
	Plants with goodly burden bowing.

Ferdinand compliments Prospero on how amazing the show is. Iris brings in more spirits acting as farm workers and nymphs who dance together.

Goddesses, Miranda and Ferdinand, 2006

Activity 5: Exploring staging

a. In groups, read aloud the **stage direction** after line 138.
b. Now read aloud lines 134–145, swapping reader at each punctuation mark.
c. Decide who will play Prospero, Iris, Miranda, Ferdinand and the spirits. Then create a **freeze-frame** of lines 134–138.
d. Create a second freeze-frame showing lines 143–145.
e. On your feet, using the stage directions to help you, work out how you might stage the action between your two freeze-frames.
f. Create a performance of lines 134–145 that begins with the first freeze-frame, comes to life, then ends with the second freeze-frame.
g. Imagine you are either Ferdinand or Miranda. Describe the events of lines 134–145, including what you saw and how you felt about what happened.

Glossary

128 **Naiads** water nymphs
128 **windring** winding and wandering
129 **sedged** made from grasses
130 **crisp channels** rippling streams
132 **temperate** gentle; chaste
134 **sicklemen** farm workers cutting the crops
135 **furrow** fields
138 **country footing** dancing

Key terms

Staging the process of selecting, adapting and developing the stage space in which a play will be performed
Stage direction an instruction in the text of a play, e.g. indicating which characters enter and exit a scene
Freeze-frame a physical, still image created by people to represent an object, place, person or feeling

Spring come to you at the farthest,
In the very end of harvest. 115
Scarcity and want shall shun you,
Ceres' blessing so is on you.

Ferdinand   This is a most majestic vision, and
Harmonious charmingly. May I be bold
To think these spirits?

Prospero   Spirits, which by mine art , 120
I have from their confines called to enact
My present fancies.

Ferdinand   Let me live here ever.
So rare a wondered father, and a wise,
Makes this place paradise.

Juno and Ceres whisper, and send Iris on employment

Prospero   Sweet, now, silence.
Juno and Ceres whisper seriously. 125
There's something else to do. Hush, and be mute,
Or else our spell is marred.

Iris   You nymphs, called Naiads, of the windring brooks,
With your sedged crowns and ever-harmless looks,
Leave your crisp channels, and on this green land 130
Answer your summons; Juno does command.
Come, temperate nymphs, and help to celebrate
A contract of true love; be not too late.

Enter certain nymphs

You sunburned sicklemen of August weary,
Come hither from the furrow and be merry. 135
Make holiday; your rye-straw hats put on,
And these fresh nymphs encounter every one
In country footing.

*Enter certain reapers, properly habited. They join with the nymphs in
a graceful dance, towards the end whereof Prospero starts suddenly
and speaks; after which, to a strange, hollow, and confused noise, they
heavily vanish*

Prospero suddenly remembers Caliban's plot against him and ends the show. He sends Miranda and Ferdinand away and calls Ariel.

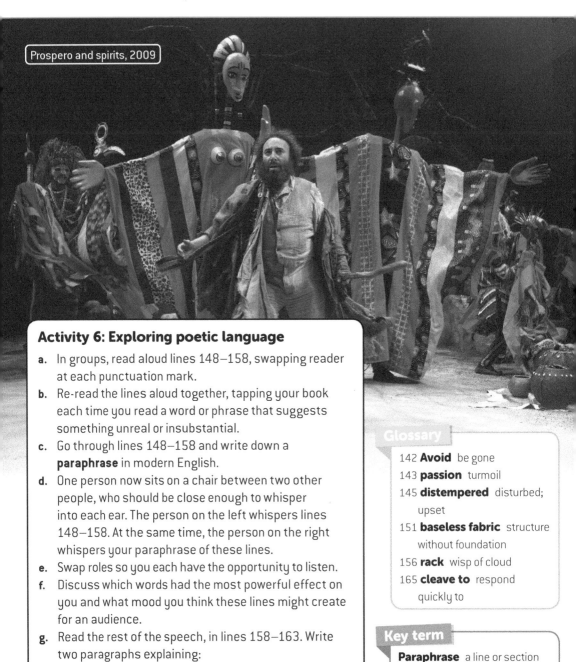

Prospero and spirits, 2009

Activity 6: Exploring poetic language

a. In groups, read aloud lines 148–158, swapping reader at each punctuation mark.
b. Re-read the lines aloud together, tapping your book each time you read a word or phrase that suggests something unreal or insubstantial.
c. Go through lines 148–158 and write down a **paraphrase** in modern English.
d. One person now sits on a chair between two other people, who should be close enough to whisper into each ear. The person on the left whispers lines 148–158. At the same time, the person on the right whispers your paraphrase of these lines.
e. Swap roles so you each have the opportunity to listen.
f. Discuss which words had the most powerful effect on you and what mood you think these lines might create for an audience.
g. Read the rest of the speech, in lines 158–163. Write two paragraphs explaining:
   • how you think Prospero feels as he speaks
   • how an audience might feel listening to him.

Glossary
142 **Avoid** be gone
143 **passion** turmoil
145 **distempered** disturbed; upset
151 **baseless fabric** structure without foundation
156 **rack** wisp of cloud
165 **cleave to** respond quickly to

Key term
Paraphrase a line or section of text expressed in your own words

Prospero [Aside] I had forgot that foul conspiracy
Of the beast Caliban and his confederates   140
Against my life. The minute of their plot
Is almost come. [To the spirits] Well done. Avoid. No more!

Exeunt spirits

Ferdinand This is strange. Your father's in some passion
That works him strongly.

Miranda   Never till this day
Saw I him touched with anger, so distempered.   145

Prospero You do look, my son, in a movèd sort,
As if you were dismayed. Be cheerful, sir.
Our revels now are ended. These our actors,
As I foretold you, were all spirits and
Are melted into air, into thin air,   150
And, like the baseless fabric of this vision,
The cloud-capped towers, the gorgeous palaces,
The solemn temples, the great globe itself,
Yea, all which it inherit, shall dissolve,
And, like this insubstantial pageant faded,   155
Leave not a rack behind. We are such stuff
As dreams are made on; and our little life
Is rounded with a sleep. Sir, I am vexed,
Bear with my weakness, my old brain is troubled.
Be not disturbed with my infirmity,   160
If you be pleased, retire into my cell
And there repose. A turn or two I'll walk
To still my beating mind.

Ferdinand & Miranda   We wish your peace.

Exeunt Ferdinand and Miranda

Prospero Come with a thought; I thank thee, Ariel. Come!

Enter Ariel

Ariel Thy thoughts I cleave to. What's thy pleasure?   165

Ariel reports to Prospero how he used his music to charm Caliban, Stephano and Trinculo, and lead them through briars and gorse bushes, leaving them in a dirty stagnant pool. Prospero praises him and tells him to bring some fine clothes that will attract their attention.

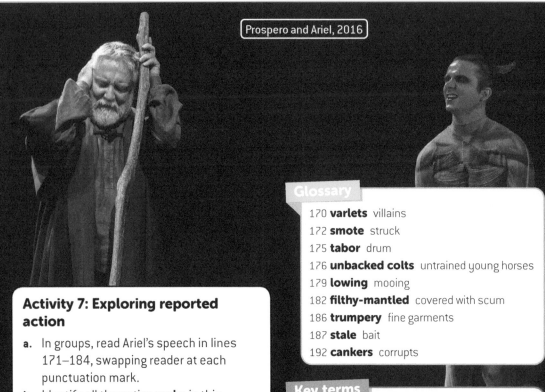

Prospero and Ariel, 2016

Glossary

170 **varlets** villains
172 **smote** struck
175 **tabor** drum
176 **unbacked colts** untrained young horses
179 **lowing** mooing
182 **filthy-mantled** covered with scum
186 **trumpery** fine garments
187 **stale** bait
192 **cankers** corrupts

Activity 7: Exploring reported action

a. In groups, read Ariel's speech in lines 171–184, swapping reader at each punctuation mark.
b. Identify all the action **verbs** in this speech and agree an understanding of what each means.
c. Repeat task a, this time adding an appropriate gesture every time you say a verb.
d. Now one or more of you play Ariel and read aloud the speech as the others act out everything Ariel describes. The readers should be loud and clear so that the actors can hear them and they should watch the actors so that they can pace their reading to support the performance.
e. Discuss how this activity brought out the humour of Ariel's story.

Key terms

Verb a word describing an action or a state, e.g. *jump*, *shout*, *believe*, *exist*
Theme the main ideas explored in a piece of literature, e.g. the themes of power and authority, hope and fear, family, vengeance and forgiveness might be considered key themes of *The Tempest*

Activity 8: Exploring the theme of forgiveness

a. Read Prospero's speech in lines 188–193 and paraphrase it.
b. How likely do you think Prospero is to forgive Caliban for his behaviour?

Prospero	Spirit, we must prepare to meet with Caliban.
Ariel	Ay, my commander. When I presented Ceres, I thought to have told thee of it, but I feared Lest I might anger thee.
Prospero	Say again, where didst thou leave these varlets?
Ariel	I told you, sir, they were red-hot with drinking, So full of valour that they smote the air For breathing in their faces, beat the ground For kissing of their feet; yet always bending Towards their project. Then I beat my tabor, At which, like unbacked colts, they pricked their ears, Advanced their eyelids, lifted up their noses As they smelt music. So I charmed their ears, That calf-like they my lowing followed through Toothed briars, sharp furzes, pricking gorse and thorns, Which entered their frail shins. At last I left them I'th' filthy-mantled pool beyond your cell, There dancing up to th'chins, that the foul lake O'erstunk their feet.
Prospero	This was well done, my bird. Thy shape invisible retain thou still. The trumpery in my house, go bring it hither For stale to catch these thieves.
Ariel	I go, I go.

Exit Ariel

Prospero	A devil, a born devil, on whose nature Nurture can never stick; on whom my pains, Humanely taken, all, all lost, quite lost. And as with age his body uglier grows, So his mind cankers. I will plague them all, Even to roaring.

Enter Ariel, laden with glistering apparel, etc.

Come, hang them on this line.

170

175

180

185

190

Caliban leads Stephano and Trinculo towards Prospero's cell. Stephano and Trinculo complain about being wet and smelly and losing their bottle of wine. Caliban urges them to be quiet. Stephano is ready to kill Prospero but then they see an array of fine clothes.

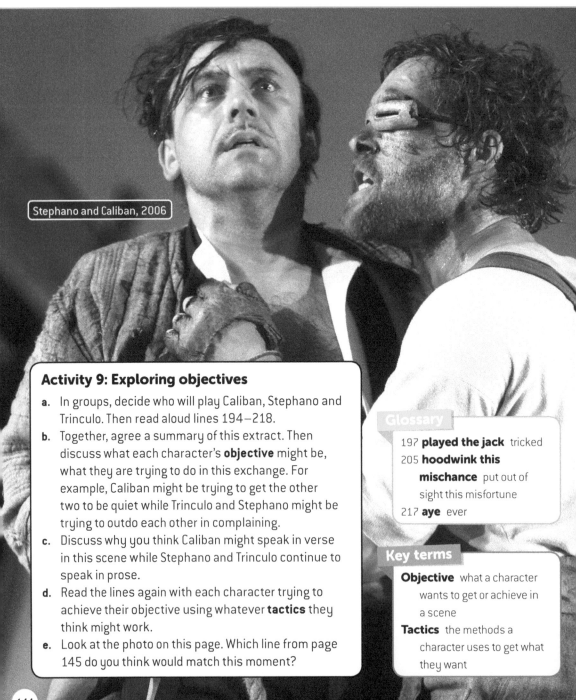

Stephano and Caliban, 2006

Activity 9: Exploring objectives

a. In groups, decide who will play Caliban, Stephano and Trinculo. Then read aloud lines 194–218.

b. Together, agree a summary of this extract. Then discuss what each character's **objective** might be, what they are trying to do in this exchange. For example, Caliban might be trying to get the other two to be quiet while Trinculo and Stephano might be trying to outdo each other in complaining.

c. Discuss why you think Caliban might speak in verse in this scene while Stephano and Trinculo continue to speak in prose.

d. Read the lines again with each character trying to achieve their objective using whatever **tactics** they think might work.

e. Look at the photo on this page. Which line from page 145 do you think would match this moment?

Glossary

197 **played the jack** tricked
205 **hoodwink this mischance** put out of sight this misfortune
217 **aye** ever

Key terms

Objective what a character wants to get or achieve in a scene

Tactics the methods a character uses to get what they want

Prospero and Ariel remain, invisible. Enter Caliban, Stephano and Trinculo,
all wet

Caliban	Pray you, tread softly, that the blind mole may
	Not hear a foot fall. We now are near his cell. 195
Stephano	Monster, your fairy, which you say is a harmless fairy, has done
	little better than played the jack with us.
Trinculo	Monster, I do smell all horse-piss, at which my nose is in great
	indignation.
Stephano	So is mine. Do you hear, monster? If I should take a displeasure 200
	against you, look you—
Trinculo	Thou wert but a lost monster.
Caliban	Good my lord, give me thy favour still.
	Be patient, for the prize I'll bring thee to
	Shall hoodwink this mischance; therefore speak softly, 205
	All's hushed as midnight yet.
Trinculo	Ay, but to lose our bottles in the pool!
Stephano	There is not only disgrace and dishonour in that, monster, but an
	infinite loss.
Trinculo	That's more to me than my wetting. Yet this is your harmless fairy, 210
	monster.
Stephano	I will fetch off my bottle, though I be o'er ears for my labour.
Caliban	Prithee, my king, be quiet. Seest thou here,
	This is the mouth o'th'cell. No noise, and enter.
	Do that good mischief which may make this island 215
	Thine own forever, and I thy Caliban
	For aye thy foot-licker.
Stephano	Give me thy hand. I do begin to have bloody thoughts.
Trinculo	O King Stephano, O peer. O worthy Stephano, look what a
	wardrobe here is for thee. 220
Caliban	Let it alone, thou fool, it is but trash.

Trinculo and Stephano delightedly gather up the fine clothes. Caliban tries to stop them and get them to stick to their plan to kill Prospero before he wakes up. Suddenly a noise of hunting is heard.

Stephano, 2016

Activity 10: Exploring the theme of hope and fear

a. In groups, decide who will play Caliban, Stephano and Trinculo. Then read aloud lines 222–247.

b. Discuss what each character's objective might be in this exchange. Have the objectives changed since page 145?

c. Look through the lines again and reduce this exchange to just 12 words. These 12 words can come from anywhere in lines 222–247 and can be next to each other.

d. In your group, create a performance of this moment in the play, using only your 12 words, accompanied by actions and gestures. Make sure that your words and actions tell the story of what happens clearly and that everyone in the scene responds to the words and actions of the other characters.

e. Imagine Caliban turns to address the audience as Stephano and Trinculo take the clothes. Write a **monologue** for Caliban in which he describes the hopes and fears running through his mind at this moment.

Glossary

223 **frippery** second-hand clothes shop

226 **dropsy** a disease

231 **Mistress line** he addresses the clothes line

231 **jerkin** jacket

232 **under the line** off the clothes line

234 **line and level** methodically

237 **pass of pate** exchange of wit

238 **lime** sticky substance spread on trees to catch small birds

244 **hogshead** large cask

Key term

Monologue a long speech in which a character expresses their thoughts. Other characters may be present

Trinculo	[Putting on a gown] O, ho, monster, we know what belongs to a frippery. O, King Stephano!
Stephano	Put off that gown, Trinculo. By this hand, I'll have that gown.
Trinculo	Thy grace shall have it. 225
Caliban	The dropsy drown this fool. What do you mean To dote thus on such luggage? Let's alone And do the murder first. If he awake, From toe to crown he'll fill our skins with pinches, Make us strange stuff. 230
Stephano	Be you quiet, monster. Mistress line, is not this my jerkin? Now is the jerkin under the line. Now, jerkin, you are like to lose your hair and prove a bald jerkin.
	Stephano and Trinculo take garments
Trinculo	Do, do; we steal by line and level, and it like your grace.
Stephano	I thank thee for that jest. Here's a garment for it. Wit shall not go 235 unrewarded while I am king of this country. 'Steal by line and level' is an excellent pass of pate. There's another garment for it.
Trinculo	Monster, come put some lime upon your fingers, and away with the rest.
Caliban	I will have none on't. We shall lose our time, 240 And all be turned to barnacles, or to apes With foreheads villainous low.
Stephano	Monster, lay to your fingers. Help to bear this away where my hogshead of wine is, or I'll turn you out of my kingdom. [Loading Caliban with garments] Go to, carry this. 245
Trinculo	And this.
Stephano	Ay, and this.
	A noise of hunters heard. Enter diverse spirits, in shape of dogs and hounds, hunting them about, Prospero and Ariel setting them on

147

Prospero and Ariel enter with the spirits of the island as hunting dogs, which chase Caliban, Stephano and Trinculo. Prospero orders that the spirits ensure the conspirators suffer pain and announces that now all his enemies are at his mercy.

Ariel (above), Stephano, Caliban, Trinculo and spirits, 2016

Activity 11: Exploring atmosphere

a. As with the gods' blessing, how to show the hounds in this scene is also a challenge for directors of this play. What kind of atmosphere do you think this scene should create for the audience? Discuss all the ideas you can think of for creating that atmosphere, using sound, lighting, **props** and costumes.

b. Look at the photo on this page. How did this production create an atmosphere and how effective do you think it might have been?

Glossary

251 **dry convulsions** painful cramps
252 **agèd cramps** the pains of old age
252 **pinch-spotted** covered in spots; bruised
253 **pard** leopard

Key term

Prop an object used in the play, e.g. a dagger

Prospero	Hey, Mountain, hey!
Ariel	Silver! There it goes, Silver!
Prospero	Fury, Fury! There, Tyrant, there! Hark, hark!

Exeunt Caliban, Stephano and Trinculo, pursued by spirits

[To Ariel] Go, charge my goblins that they grind their joints 250
With dry convulsions, shorten up their sinews
With agèd cramps, and more pinch-spotted make them
Than pard or cat o'mountain.

Ariel	Hark, they roar.

Prospero Let them be hunted soundly. At this hour
Lies at my mercy all mine enemies. 255
Shortly shall all my labours end, and thou
Shalt have the air at freedom. For a little,
Follow, and do me service.

Exeunt

Exploring Act 4

Iris, Ferdinand, Juno, Miranda and Ceres, 2016

Activity 1: Exploring the theme of family in Act 4

a. In pairs, draw a family tree each for Miranda and for Ferdinand. Use page 15 to help you as well as your knowledge of the play so far. Add any other family members you think appropriate, for example, their mothers.

b. Discuss the extent to which Miranda might consider Caliban as part of her family.

c. Consider how each character's family background and upbringing might have influenced their attitudes to life.

d. Now imagine one of you is Miranda and the other is Ferdinand. **Improvise** a conversation where you ask each other about your families, using the family trees to help you but filling in personal details about your memories and feelings about your family and upbringing.

e. Imagine you are an actor preparing to audition for the role of either Ferdinand or Miranda in a new production of *The Tempest*. The director has asked you to think particularly about the character's upbringing. Using your ideas from tasks a–d, write notes under the following headings to help you prepare for the role:
   i.   Relationship with father
   ii. Relationship with mother
   iii. Relationship with other significant family members
   iv. Attitude to life (summary of my character's personality and evidence in the text that led me to think that)
   v.   Links and gaps (what I have in common with my character and what I don't but will have to imagine).

Key term

Improvise   make up in the moment

Activity 2: Exploring the events of Act 4

a. In groups, look back through Act 4 and agree on three or four moments that seem the most important. Use the page summaries to help you.

b. Choose one or two lines of text for each of your moments.

c. Create three or four freeze-frames, showing each of your moments and include a way of speaking your chosen lines of text aloud in your freeze-frames.

d. Record your freeze-frames by photographing, drawing or describing them. Give each one your chosen line as a title. Under each image explain:
   - why you feel this moment is important
   - why you chose this line of text for this moment
   - how your freeze-frame portrays this moment and line effectively.

Prospero reviews the progress of his plans. Ariel tells him that the nobles are all imprisoned under his spell and are so unhappy that they inspire pity. Prospero agrees.

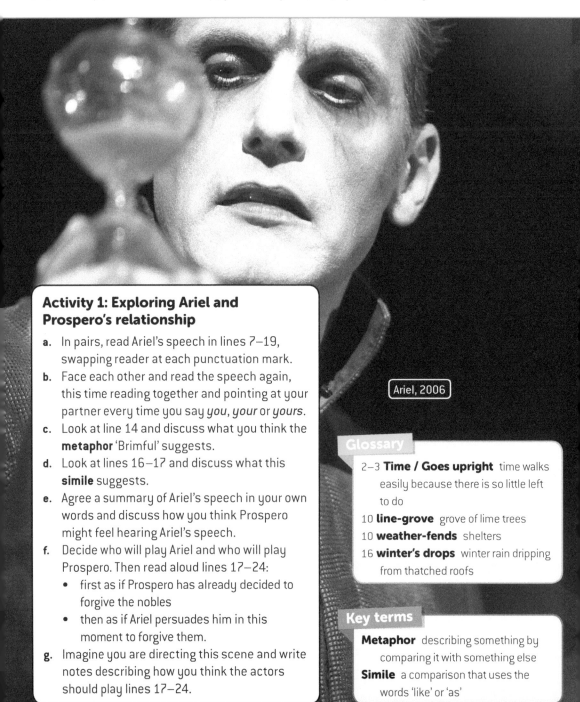

Ariel, 2006

Activity 1: Exploring Ariel and Prospero's relationship

a. In pairs, read Ariel's speech in lines 7–19, swapping reader at each punctuation mark.

b. Face each other and read the speech again, this time reading together and pointing at your partner every time you say *you*, *your* or *yours*.

c. Look at line 14 and discuss what you think the **metaphor** 'Brimful' suggests.

d. Look at lines 16–17 and discuss what this **simile** suggests.

e. Agree a summary of Ariel's speech in your own words and discuss how you think Prospero might feel hearing Ariel's speech.

f. Decide who will play Ariel and who will play Prospero. Then read aloud lines 17–24:
  - first as if Prospero has already decided to forgive the nobles
  - then as if Ariel persuades him in this moment to forgive them.

g. Imagine you are directing this scene and write notes describing how you think the actors should play lines 17–24.

Glossary

2–3 **Time / Goes upright** time walks easily because there is so little left to do

10 **line-grove** grove of lime trees

10 **weather-fends** shelters

16 **winter's drops** winter rain dripping from thatched roofs

Key terms

Metaphor describing something by comparing it with something else

Simile a comparison that uses the words 'like' or 'as'

Enter Prospero in his magic robes, and Ariel

Prospero Now does my project gather to a head.
My charms crack not, my spirits obey, and Time
Goes upright with his carriage. How's the day?

Ariel On the sixth hour, at which time, my lord,
You said our work should cease.

Prospero   I did say so,   5
When first I raised the tempest. Say, my spirit,
How fares the king and's followers?

Ariel   Confined together
In the same fashion as you gave in charge,
Just as you left them; all prisoners, sir,
In the line-grove which weather-fends your cell.   10
They cannot budge till your release. The king,
His brother, and yours abide all three distracted,
And the remainder mourning over them,
Brimful of sorrow and dismay. But chiefly
Him that you termed, sir, the good old lord Gonzalo,   15
His tears run down his beard, like winter's drops
From eaves of reeds. Your charm so strongly works 'em
That if you now beheld them, your affections
Would become tender.

Prospero   Dost thou think so, spirit?

Ariel Mine would, sir, were I human.

Prospero   And mine shall.   20
Hast thou, which art but air, a touch, a feeling
Of their afflictions, and shall not myself,
One of their kind, that relish all as sharply
Passion as they, be kindlier moved than thou art?

Prospero tells Ariel he will forgive the nobles if they are sorry for how they treated him. Ariel goes to get them. Prospero describes his magical powers to the audience but says he will give them up.

Prospero, 2009

At the time

Using page 190, find out more about Shakespeare's sources for this play. One of the writers Shakespeare was very inspired by was called Ovid. He died in AD17 and wrote stories that Shakespeare used as starting points for his plays. In one of the stories, Ovid also had a powerful witch who spoke words similar to these. The speech on page 155 is similar to this speech. What effect do you think this speech might have had on the audience in Shakespeare's time compared to our own?

Glossary

27 **rarer** unusual, deeper
28 **penitent** sorry
35 **ebbing Neptune** receding tide. Neptune was Roman god of the sea
36 **demi-puppets** tiny fairies
37 **green sour ringlets** dark green rings in the grass thought to be made by fairies dancing
40 **solemn curfew** nine o'clock bell indicating spirits are free to roam until dawn
41 **bedimmed** clouded over
43 **azured vault** blue sky
45 **rifted** split
46 **bolt** lightning. Jove was Roman god of lightning
47 **spurs** roots
51 **abjure** reject

Activity 2: Exploring language

a. In groups, read aloud Prospero's speech in lines 33–57.
b. Read the speech again, swapping reader at each full stop or semi-colon.
c. Repeat task b, this time only the person reading should look at the page. The others in your group should listen and repeat aloud any words that sound interesting.
d. Between you, choose seven words or phrases that you like and agree **gestures** to match those words.
e. Rehearse a performance speaking your seven words or phrases with the gestures. Share your performance with others and discuss what you liked about each other's performances.
f. Look again at the last sentence (lines 50–57) and discuss why you think Prospero makes this promise to the audience to give up his magic.

Key term

Gesture a movement, often using the hands or head, to express a feeling or idea

Though with their high wrongs I am struck to th'quick,   25
Yet with my nobler reason 'gainst my fury
Do I take part. The rarer action is
In virtue than in vengeance. They being penitent,
The sole drift of my purpose doth extend
Not a frown further. Go, release them, Ariel.   30
My charms I'll break, their senses I'll restore,
And they shall be themselves.

Ariel   I'll fetch them, sir.

Exit Ariel

Prospero Ye elves of hills, brooks, standing lakes and groves,
And ye that on the sands with printless foot
Do chase the ebbing Neptune, and do fly him   35
When he comes back. You demi-puppets that
By moonshine do the green sour ringlets make,
Whereof the ewe not bites; and you whose pastime
Is to make midnight mushrumps, that rejoice
To hear the solemn curfew, by whose aid,   40
Weak masters though ye be, I have bedimmed
The noontide sun, called forth the mutinous winds,
And 'twixt the green sea and the azured vault
Set roaring war. To the dread rattling thunder
Have I given fire, and rifted Jove's stout oak   45
With his own bolt. The strong-based promontory
Have I made shake and by the spurs plucked up
The pine and cedar. Graves at my command
Have waked their sleepers, oped, and let 'em forth
By my so potent art. But this rough magic   50
I here abjure; and when I have required
Some heavenly music, which even now I do,
To work mine end upon their senses that
This airy charm is for, I'll break my staff,
Bury it certain fathoms in the earth,   55
And deeper than did ever plummet sound
I'll drown my book.

Ariel leads in the nobles who are all under a spell. Prospero forgives them and sends Ariel to fetch the clothes he wore when he was Duke of Milan so that they will recognise him when they come to their senses again.

Prospero, Ariel, Alonso, Gonzalo, Antonio, Adrian and Sebastian, 2009

Activity 3: Exploring the theme of vengeance and forgiveness

a. In groups, read aloud lines 68–79.
b. Decide who will play Prospero, Gonzalo, Alonso, Sebastian and Antonio. Then create a **freeze-frame** of this moment.
c. 'Prospero' comes to life from this freeze-frame and speaks lines 68–79 to the appropriate characters in turn.
d. Discuss how you think each character might respond if they knew how Prospero had controlled them. Would they want revenge on him? Would they be fearful of his powers? Would they ask for forgiveness for how they treated him in the past?
e. Agree a one-line response in your own words from each character to Prospero.
f. Create a performance of this moment that begins with your freeze-frame, brings it to life with Prospero speaking lines 68–79 and the others responding with their lines, and then ends on a final freeze-frame that shows clearly how each character feels about Prospero.

Glossary

59 **unsettled fancy** disturbed imagination
59 **cure** soothe; make better
63 **sociable** sympathetic
67 **mantle** cloak
70 **graces** good deeds
84 **rapier** sword
85 **discase** undress; change costume
86 **As I was sometime Milan** as I formerly appeared as the Duke of Milan

Key terms

Theme the main ideas explored in a piece of literature, e.g. the themes of power and authority, hope and fear, family, vengeance and forgiveness might be considered key themes of The Tempest

Freeze-frame a physical, still image created by people to represent an object, place, person or feeling

Solemn music. Here enters Ariel before. Then Alonso, with a frantic
gesture, attended by Gonzalo, Sebastian and Antonio in like manner,
attended by Adrian and Francisco. They all enter the circle which Prospero
had made, and there stand charmed, which Prospero observing, speaks

A solemn air, and the best comforter
To an unsettled fancy, cure thy brains,
Now useless, boil within thy skull. There stand,   60
For you are spell-stopped.
Holy Gonzalo, honourable man,
Mine eyes, even sociable to the show of thine,
Fall fellowly drops. The charm dissolves apace,
And as the morning steals upon the night,   65
Melting the darkness, so their rising senses
Begin to chase the ignorant fumes that mantle
Their clearer reason. O good Gonzalo,
My true preserver, and a loyal sir
To him thou follow'st, I will pay thy graces   70
Home both in word and deed. Most cruelly
Didst thou, Alonso, use me and my daughter.
Thy brother was a furtherer in the act.
Thou art pinched for't now, Sebastian. Flesh and blood,
You, brother mine, that entertain ambition,   75
Expelled remorse and nature; who, with Sebastian,
Whose inward pinches therefore are most strong,
Would here have killed your king, I do forgive thee,
Unnatural though thou art. Their understanding
Begins to swell, and the approaching tide   80
Will shortly fill the reasonable shore
That now lies foul and muddy. Not one of them
That yet looks on me or would know me. Ariel,
Fetch me the hat and rapier in my cell.
I will discase me, and myself present   85
As I was sometime Milan. Quickly, spirit!
Thou shalt ere long be free.

Ariel sings and helps to attire him

Ariel   Where the bee sucks, there suck I.

Prospero promises Ariel his freedom for his service and sends him to bring the master and the Boatswain from the king's ship. Prospero announces himself to the nobles. Alonso acknowledges him as the real Prospero and gives him back his dukedom.

Prospero and Ariel, 2012

Prospero and Ariel, 2016

Activity 4: Exploring Ariel

a. Look at lines 95–96 and discuss what you think Prospero will miss about Ariel.

b. Ariel is a magical creature so can be played in many different ways. Look at the examples in the photos on this page and elsewhere in the book, and discuss the different ways Ariel is portrayed.

c. Imagine you are the director for a production of the play. Write notes for your **casting** director about the kind of actor you want to play Ariel. Include:
- a summary of Ariel's personality
- ideas on how he should look and sound
- examples of famous actors who could play your Ariel.

Glossary

89 **cowslip's bell** the petals of the small yellow flower

90 **couch** rest

94 **bough** branch

112 **enchanted trifle** illusion; trick

115 **amends** improves

116 **crave** require

Did you know?

Ariel has been performed in many ways in different productions of *The Tempest*. From the early 18th century until the early 19th century, Ariel was most commonly played by women. Sometimes Ariel is played as very energetic and agile, and sometimes as very still and mysterious.

Key term

Casting deciding which actors should play which roles

In a cowslip's bell I lie.
There I couch when owls do cry.   90
On the bat's back I do fly
After summer merrily.
Merrily, merrily shall I live now
Under the blossom that hangs on the bough.

Prospero   Why, that's my dainty Ariel. I shall miss thee,   95
But yet thou shalt have freedom. So, so, so.
To the king's ship, invisible as thou art.
There shalt thou find the mariners asleep
Under the hatches. The master and the boatswain
Being awake, enforce them to this place,   100
And presently, I prithee.

Ariel   I drink the air before me, and return
Or ere your pulse twice beat.

Exit Ariel

Gonzalo   All torment, trouble, wonder, and amazement
Inhabits here. Some heavenly power guide us   105
Out of this fearful country!

Prospero   Behold, sir king,
The wrongèd Duke of Milan, Prospero.
For more assurance that a living prince
Does now speak to thee, I embrace thy body,
And to thee and thy company, I bid   110
A hearty welcome.

He embraces Alonso

Alonso   Whe'er thou beest he or no,
Or some enchanted trifle to abuse me,
As late I have been, I not know. Thy pulse
Beats as of flesh and blood; and since I saw thee
The affliction of my mind amends, with which   115
I fear a madness held me. This must crave,
And if this be at all, a most strange story.
Thy dukedom I resign, and do entreat

Prospero embraces Gonzalo and assures him he will feel back to normal soon. He warns Sebastian and Antonio that he knows about their plot against Alonso but will keep quiet for now. Alonso asks how Prospero ended up on the same island they were shipwrecked on, and mourns the loss of Ferdinand.

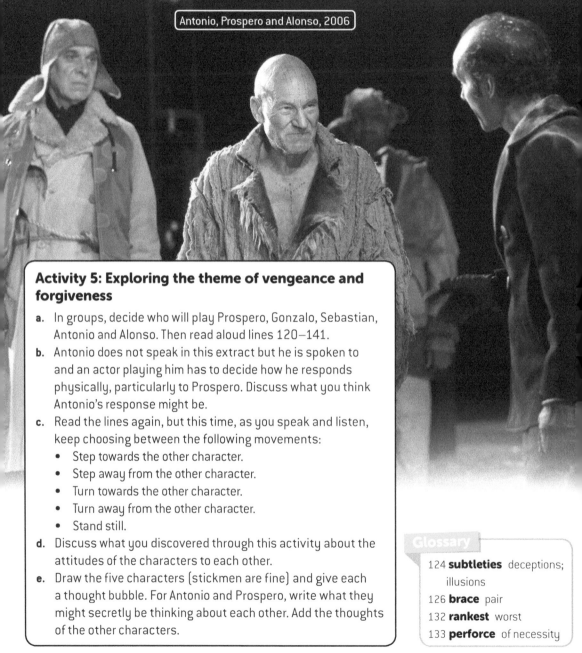

Antonio, Prospero and Alonso, 2006

Activity 5: Exploring the theme of vengeance and forgiveness

a. In groups, decide who will play Prospero, Gonzalo, Sebastian, Antonio and Alonso. Then read aloud lines 120–141.

b. Antonio does not speak in this extract but he is spoken to and an actor playing him has to decide how he responds physically, particularly to Prospero. Discuss what you think Antonio's response might be.

c. Read the lines again, but this time, as you speak and listen, keep choosing between the following movements:
- Step towards the other character.
- Step away from the other character.
- Turn towards the other character.
- Turn away from the other character.
- Stand still.

d. Discuss what you discovered through this activity about the attitudes of the characters to each other.

e. Draw the five characters (stickmen are fine) and give each a thought bubble. For Antonio and Prospero, write what they might secretly be thinking about each other. Add the thoughts of the other characters.

Glossary
124 **subtleties** deceptions; illusions
126 **brace** pair
132 **rankest** worst
133 **perforce** of necessity

Thou pardon me my wrongs. But how should Prospero
Be living and be here?

Prospero   [To Gonzalo] First, noble friend,   120
Let me embrace thine age, whose honour cannot
Be measured or confined.

He embraces Gonzalo

Gonzalo   Whether this be
Or be not, I'll not swear.

Prospero   You do yet taste
Some subtleties o'th'isle, that will not let you
Believe things certain. Welcome, my friends all.   125
[Aside to Sebastian and Antonio]
But you, my brace of lords, were I so minded,
I here could pluck his highness' frown upon you,
And justify you traitors. At this time,
I will tell no tales.

Sebastian   The devil speaks in him.

Prospero   No.
For you, most wicked sir, whom to call brother   130
Would even infect my mouth, I do forgive
Thy rankest fault, all of them, and require
My dukedom of thee, which perforce I know
Thou must restore.

Alonso   If thou beest Prospero,
Give us particulars of thy preservation.   135
How thou hast met us here, whom three hours since
Were wrecked upon this shore? Where I have lost,
How sharp the point of this remembrance is,
My dear son Ferdinand.

Prospero   I am woe for it, sir.

Alonso   Irreparable is the loss, and patience   140
Says it is past her cure.

Prospero tells Alonso he has also suffered a loss, having lost his daughter in the tempest. Alonso wishes they could have been king and queen of Naples. Prospero promises to tell them his full story but in the meantime has something to offer in return for his dukedom. He reveals Miranda and Ferdinand playing chess together.

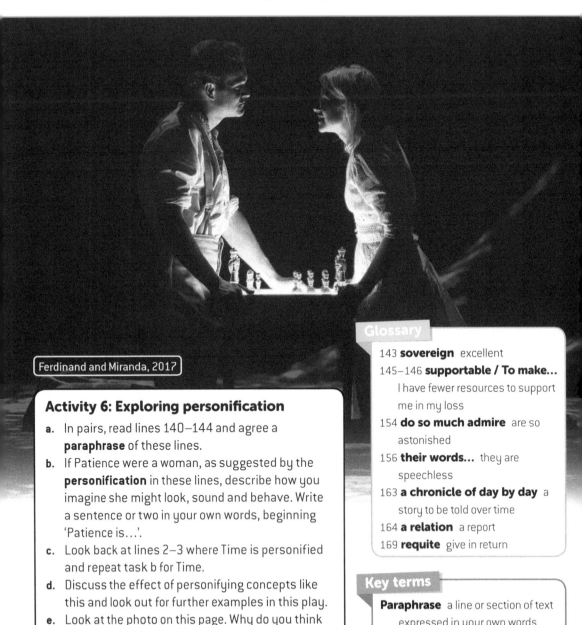

Ferdinand and Miranda, 2017

Activity 6: Exploring personification

a. In pairs, read lines 140–144 and agree a **paraphrase** of these lines.

b. If Patience were a woman, as suggested by the **personification** in these lines, describe how you imagine she might look, sound and behave. Write a sentence or two in your own words, beginning 'Patience is…'.

c. Look back at lines 2–3 where Time is personified and repeat task b for Time.

d. Discuss the effect of personifying concepts like this and look out for further examples in this play.

e. Look at the photo on this page. Why do you think Shakespeare has Miranda and Ferdinand play chess?

Glossary

143 **sovereign** excellent

145–146 **supportable / To make…** I have fewer resources to support me in my loss

154 **do so much admire** are so astonished

156 **their words…** they are speechless

163 **a chronicle of day by day** a story to be told over time

164 **a relation** a report

169 **requite** give in return

Key terms

Paraphrase a line or section of text expressed in your own words

Personification giving an object or concept human qualities

Prospero
                            I rather think
You have not sought her help, of whose soft grace
For the like loss, I have her sovereign aid,
And rest myself content.

Alonso
                         You the like loss?

Prospero
As great to me as late, and supportable   145
To make the dear loss have I means much weaker
Than you may call to comfort you; for I
Have lost my daughter.

Alonso
                      A daughter?
O heavens, that they were living both in Naples,
The king and queen there. That they were, I wish   150
Myself were mudded in that oozy bed
Where my son lies. When did you lose your daughter?

Prospero
In this last tempest. I perceive these lords
At this encounter do so much admire
That they devour their reason and scarce think   155
Their eyes do offices of truth; their words
Are natural breath. But, howsoe'er you have
Been jostled from your senses, know for certain
That I am Prospero, and that very duke
Which was thrust forth of Milan, who most strangely   160
Upon this shore, where you were wrecked, was landed
To be the lord on't. No more yet of this,
For 'tis a chronicle of day by day,
Not a relation for a breakfast, nor
Befitting this first meeting. Welcome, sir.   165
This cell's my court. Here have I few attendants,
And subjects none abroad. Pray you look in.
My dukedom since you have given me again,
I will requite you with as good a thing,
At least bring forth a wonder, to content ye   170
As much as me my dukedom.

Here Prospero discovers Ferdinand and Miranda playing at chess

Alonso and Ferdinand are delighted to be reunited. Miranda is amazed to see so many people. Ferdinand introduces her as his fiancée.

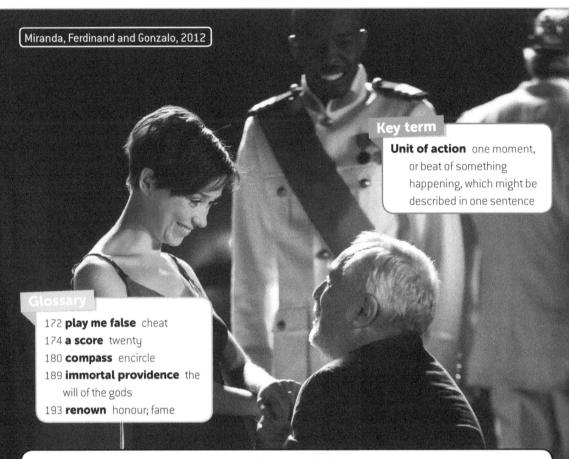

Miranda, Ferdinand and Gonzalo, 2012

Glossary

172 **play me false** cheat
174 **a score** twenty
180 **compass** encircle
189 **immortal providence** the will of the gods
193 **renown** honour; fame

Activity 7: Exploring the theme of hope and fear

a. In groups, decide who will play Miranda, Ferdinand, Alonso, Sebastian and Prospero. Then read aloud lines 177–196.
b. Divide this extract into three or four **units of action** and give each unit a title in modern English.
c. Create a freeze-frame for each unit.
d. Choose one or two words or phrases spoken by each character that might express hope.
e. Rehearse your freeze-frame sequence, finding a way to move smoothly between each one.
f. Add your words and phrases to this sequence, deciding which words to speak in which freeze-frame.
g. Share your performance with another group and discuss the moments you thought worked particularly well in each other's performances.
h. Write a paragraph from the point of view of the character you played, describing the events of this extract and your hopes and fears in this moment.

Miranda	Sweet lord, you play me false.
Ferdinand	No, my dearest love, I would not for the world.
Miranda	Yes, for a score of kingdoms you should wrangle, And I would call it fair play.
Alonso	If this prove 175 A vision of the island, one dear son Shall I twice lose.
Sebastian	A most high miracle.
Ferdinand	Though the seas threaten, they are merciful. I have cursed them without cause.

He kneels

Alonso	Now all the blessings Of a glad father compass thee about. 180 Arise, and say how thou cam'st here.
Miranda	O wonder! How many goodly creatures are there here? How beauteous mankind is! O brave new world, That has such people in't.
Prospero	'Tis new to thee.
Alonso	[To Ferdinand] What is this maid with whom thou wast at play? 185 Your eldest acquaintance cannot be three hours. Is she the goddess that hath severed us, And brought us thus together?
Ferdinand	Sir, she is mortal. But by immortal providence, she's mine. I chose her when I could not ask my father 190 For his advice, nor thought I had one. She Is daughter to this famous Duke of Milan, Of whom so often I have heard renown, But never saw before; of whom I have Received a second life, and second father 195 This lady makes him to me.

Gonzalo expresses his joy that Miranda is to become Queen of Naples and his amazement at how everything has turned out. Alonso agrees. The Master and Boatswain of the ship are led in by Ariel.

Activity 8: Exploring the theme of family

a. In groups, look at the photo on this page and identify which actor you think is playing which character.

b. Which line do you think is being spoken at this moment?

c. Recreate the image as best you can with the people in your group. Then speak aloud in modern English the thoughts of your character at this moment.

d. If you were a director of this play, how would you want your audience to feel about this family reunion? Is it a moment of joy or are there still doubts or concerns you would want to signal?

2016 RSC production

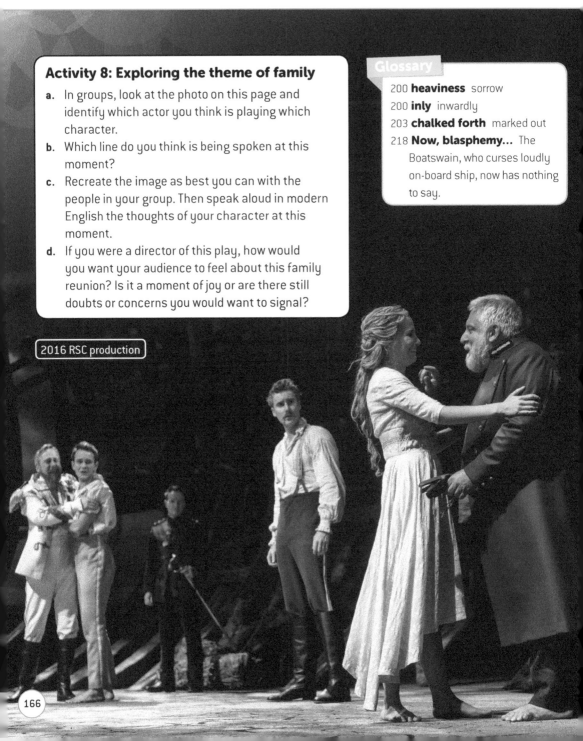

Alonso   I am hers.
But, O, how oddly will it sound that I
Must ask my child forgiveness.

Prospero   There sir, stop.
Let us not burden our remembrances with
A heaviness that's gone.

Gonzalo   I have inly wept,   200
Or should have spoke ere this. Look down you gods,
And on this couple drop a blessèd crown.
For it is you that have chalked forth the way
Which brought us hither.

Alonso   I say amen, Gonzalo.

Gonzalo Was Milan thrust from Milan that his issue   205
Should become kings of Naples? O, rejoice
Beyond a common joy, and set it down
With gold on lasting pillars. In one voyage
Did Claribel her husband find at Tunis,
And Ferdinand her brother found a wife   210
Where he himself was lost, Prospero his dukedom
In a poor isle, and all of us our selves
When no man was his own.

Alonso   [To Ferdinand and Miranda] Give me your hands.
Let grief and sorrow still embrace his heart
That doth not wish you joy.

Gonzalo   Be it so. Amen.   215

Enter Ariel, with the Master and Boatswain amazedly following

O, look, sir, look, sir! Here is more of us.
I prophesied, if a gallows were on land,
This fellow could not drown. [To Boatswain] Now, blasphemy,
That swear'st grace o'erboard, not an oath on shore?
Hast thou no mouth by land? What is the news?   220

The Boatswain describes how the crew awoke to find themselves and the ship as fit and ready to sail as when they first left home. Prospero praises Ariel for all his work and assures Alonso he will explain how all these strange events happened.

Antonio, Sebastian, Gonzalo, Alonso, Adrian, Francisco, Boatswain, Miranda and Ferdinand, 2012

Activity 9: Exploring story-telling

a. In pairs, read the Boatswain's speech in lines 229–240, swapping reader at each punctuation mark.
b. Discuss how the Boatswain's story might get the attention of the other characters, and the audience, and why. Consider:
   - how he creates tension
   - how he describes sounds, sights and feelings
   - why he tells this story in verse when we might expect him to speak prose, especially after the way Gonzalo has described him in lines 216–218.
c. Read the speech again and find ways to make the story as exciting as you can, perhaps using **pace**, **tone** and gestures.

Key terms

Pace the speed at which someone speaks
Tone as in 'tone of voice'; expressing an attitude through how you say something

Boatswain	The best news is that we have safely found
	Our king and company. The next, our ship,
	Which but three glasses since we gave out split,
	Is tight and yare and bravely rigged as when
	We first put out to sea.

Ariel   [To Prospero] Sir, all this service   225
Have I done since I went.

Prospero   [To Ariel] My tricksy spirit.

Alonso   These are not natural events, they strengthen
From strange to stranger. Say, how came you hither?

Boatswain   If I did think, sir, I were well awake,
I'd strive to tell you. We were dead of sleep,   230
And, how we know not, all clapped under hatches,
Where, but even now, with strange and several noises
Of roaring, shrieking, howling, jingling chains,
And more diversity of sounds, all horrible,
We were awaked, straightway at liberty,   235
Where we, in all our trim, freshly beheld
Our royal, good and gallant ship, our master
Capering to eye her. On a trice, so please you,
Even in a dream, were we divided from them
And were brought moping hither.

Ariel   [To Prospero] Was't well done?   240

Prospero   [To Ariel] Bravely, my diligence. Thou shalt be free.

Alonso   This is as strange a maze as e'er men trod,
And there is in this business more than nature
Was ever conduct of. Some oracle
Must rectify our knowledge.

Prospero   Sir, my liege,   245
Do not infest your mind with beating on
The strangeness of this business. At picked leisure,
Which shall be shortly, single I'll resolve you,
Which to you shall seem probable, of every

Prospero sends Ariel to free Caliban, Stephano and Trinculo. They enter and are amazed to see the others. Prospero tells the nobles that these men robbed him and plotted to kill him, and that two of them belong to Alonso's company while Caliban belongs to him.

Prospero, Boatswain and Caliban, 2009

Activity 10: Exploring the theme of power and authority

a. In pairs, read aloud Prospero's speech in lines 266–275, swapping reader at each punctuation mark.

b. Imagine one of you is Stephano and the other is Caliban. Discuss how you might feel hearing this speech.

c. Write a sentence or two each, in your own words, from the point of view of your character, summarising what you have heard Prospero say. Add a further sentence or two describing your feelings about what Prospero said and what you think will happen to you now.

d. Discuss what you think Prospero means when he says 'this thing of darkness I / Acknowledge mine.' in lines 274–275.

Glossary

250 **happened accidents** events that have taken place
256 **shift** look out
257 *Coraggio* have courage
257 **bully** a friendly term
258 **spies** eyes
260 **Setebos** a god worshipped by Sycorax
266 **badges** signs; uniform
270 **deal in her command...** control the moon without the moon's consent
271 **demi-devil** Caliban's father is said to be the devil

These happened accidents. Till when, be cheerful 250
And think of each thing well. [Aside to Ariel] Come hither, spirit,
Set Caliban and his companions free;
Untie the spell.

Exit Ariel

    [To Alonso] How fares my gracious sir?
There are yet missing of your company
Some few odd lads that you remember not. 255

Enter Ariel, driving in Caliban, Stephano and Trinculo, in their stolen apparel

Stephano   Every man shift for all the rest, and let no man take care for
himself, for all is but fortune. *Coraggio*, bully-monster, *coraggio*.

Trinculo   If these be true spies which I wear in my head, here's a goodly
sight.

Caliban   O Setebos, these be brave spirits indeed. 260
How fine my master is! I am afraid
He will chastise me.

Sebastian   Ha, ha!
What things are these, my lord Antonio?
Will money buy 'em?

Antonio   Very like. One of them
Is a plain fish, and no doubt marketable. 265

Prospero   Mark but the badges of these men, my lords,
Then say if they be true. This misshapen knave,
His mother was a witch, and one so strong
That could control the moon, make flows and ebbs,
And deal in her command without her power. 270
These three have robbed me, and this demi-devil,
For he's a bastard one, had plotted with them
To take my life. Two of these fellows you
Must know and own; this thing of darkness I
Acknowledge mine.

Alonso recognises Stephano and Trinculo, who are in a bad state. Caliban realises he was wrong to worship Stephano and is sorry. Prospero sends Caliban with Stephano and Trinculo to tidy his cell.

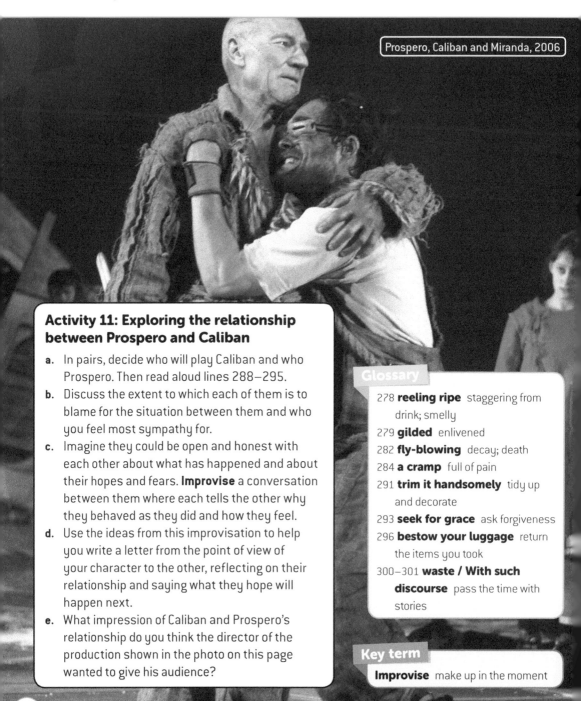

Prospero, Caliban and Miranda, 2006

Activity 11: Exploring the relationship between Prospero and Caliban

a. In pairs, decide who will play Caliban and who Prospero. Then read aloud lines 288–295.

b. Discuss the extent to which each of them is to blame for the situation between them and who you feel most sympathy for.

c. Imagine they could be open and honest with each other about what has happened and about their hopes and fears. **Improvise** a conversation between them where each tells the other why they behaved as they did and how they feel.

d. Use the ideas from this improvisation to help you write a letter from the point of view of your character to the other, reflecting on their relationship and saying what they hope will happen next.

e. What impression of Caliban and Prospero's relationship do you think the director of the production shown in the photo on this page wanted to give his audience?

Glossary

278 **reeling ripe** staggering from drink; smelly

279 **gilded** enlivened

282 **fly-blowing** decay; death

284 **a cramp** full of pain

291 **trim it handsomely** tidy up and decorate

293 **seek for grace** ask forgiveness

296 **bestow your luggage** return the items you took

300–301 **waste / With such discourse** pass the time with stories

Key term

Improvise make up in the moment

Caliban	I shall be pinched to death.	275
Alonso	Is not this Stephano, my drunken butler?	
Sebastian	He is drunk now. Where had he wine?	
Alonso	And Trinculo is reeling ripe. Where should they Find this grand liquor that hath gilded 'em? How cam'st thou in this pickle?	280
Trinculo	I have been in such a pickle since I saw you last that I fear me will never out of my bones. I shall not fear fly-blowing.	
Sebastian	Why, how now, Stephano?	
Stephano	O, touch me not. I am not Stephano, but a cramp.	
Prospero	You'd be king o'the isle, sirrah?	285
Stephano	I should have been a sore one then.	
Alonso	This is a strange thing as e'er I looked on.	
Prospero	He is as disproportioned in his manners As in his shape. Go, sirrah, to my cell. Take with you your companions. As you look To have my pardon, trim it handsomely.	290
Caliban	Ay, that I will; and I'll be wise hereafter, And seek for grace. What a thrice-double ass Was I to take this drunkard for a god! And worship this dull fool!	
Prospero	Go to, away.	295
Alonso	Hence, and bestow your luggage where you found it.	
Sebastian	Or stole it, rather.	
	Exeunt Caliban, Stephano and Trinculo	
Prospero	Sir, I invite your highness and your train To my poor cell, where you shall take your rest For this one night; which, part of it, I'll waste With such discourse as I not doubt shall make it	300

Prospero invites Alonso and the nobles to stay the night and hear his stories, then promises that good weather will take them all back to Naples the next day. Prospero sets Ariel free. He then addresses the audience, asking them to send him on his way to Naples with their applause and words of praise for the show.

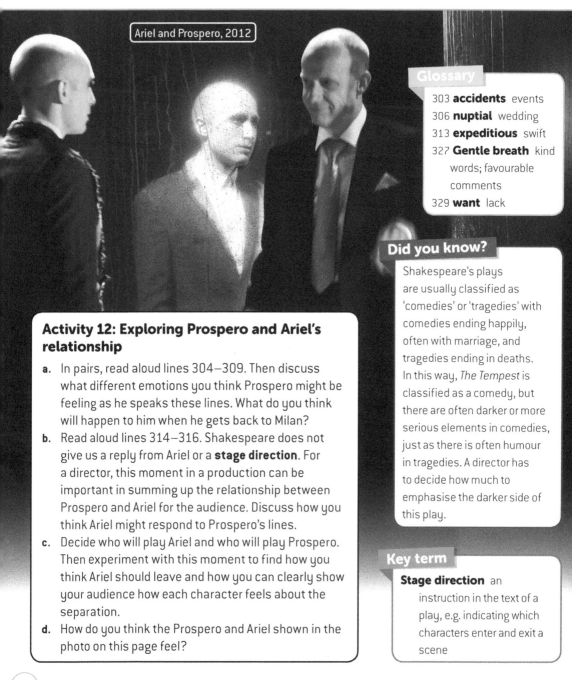

Ariel and Prospero, 2012

Did you know?

Shakespeare's plays are usually classified as 'comedies' or 'tragedies' with comedies ending happily, often with marriage, and tragedies ending in deaths. In this way, *The Tempest* is classified as a comedy, but there are often darker or more serious elements in comedies, just as there is often humour in tragedies. A director has to decide how much to emphasise the darker side of this play.

Activity 12: Exploring Prospero and Ariel's relationship

a. In pairs, read aloud lines 304–309. Then discuss what different emotions you think Prospero might be feeling as he speaks these lines. What do you think will happen to him when he gets back to Milan?

b. Read aloud lines 314–316. Shakespeare does not give us a reply from Ariel or a **stage direction**. For a director, this moment in a production can be important in summing up the relationship between Prospero and Ariel for the audience. Discuss how you think Ariel might respond to Prospero's lines.

c. Decide who will play Ariel and who will play Prospero. Then experiment with this moment to find how you think Ariel should leave and how you can clearly show your audience how each character feels about the separation.

d. How do you think the Prospero and Ariel shown in the photo on this page feel?

Key term

Stage direction an instruction in the text of a play, e.g. indicating which characters enter and exit a scene

Go quick away: the story of my life
And the particular accidents gone by
Since I came to this isle. And in the morn
I'll bring you to your ship, and so to Naples,   305
Where I have hope to see the nuptial
Of these our dear-belovèd solemnized,
And thence retire me to my Milan, where
Every third thought shall be my grave.

Alonso   I long
To hear the story of your life, which must   310
Take the ear strangely.

Prospero   I'll deliver all,
And promise you calm seas, auspicious gales
And sail so expeditious that shall catch
Your royal fleet far off. [Aside to Ariel] My Ariel, chick,
That is thy charge. Then to the elements   315
Be free, and fare thou well. Please you, draw near.

Exeunt all, except Prospero

EPILOGUE

Prospero   Now my charms are all o'erthrown,
And what strength I have's mine own,
Which is most faint. Now 'tis true,
I must be here confined by you,   320
Or sent to Naples. Let me not,
Since I have my dukedom got
And pardoned the deceiver, dwell
In this bare island by your spell,
But release me from my bands   325
With the help of your good hands.
Gentle breath of yours my sails
Must fill, or else my project fails,
Which was to please. Now I want
Spirits to enforce, art to enchant,   330
And my ending is despair,
Unless I be relieved by prayer,

Prospero appeals to the audience to set him free through their approval of the play.

Prospero, 2016

Activity 13: Exploring the epilogue

a. In pairs, read aloud Prospero's speech in lines 317–336, swapping reader at the end of each line.

b. Discuss what you notice about the use of rhythm and rhyme in this speech. Why do you think this might be different from how Prospero normally speaks?

c. How would you describe the tone of this speech?

d. Do you think that Prospero is speaking in character or is it the actor talking about performing Prospero? Try to distinguish these two different perspectives in the speech.

e. Using your responses to these questions, write a paragraph beginning 'I think Shakespeare has Prospero end the play because…'.

Glossary

333 **pierces** move deeply

336 **indulgence** approval

Did you know?

The Tempest is generally believed to be the last play Shakespeare wrote on his own. He did continue to write plays with other authors but some people believe Prospero's last speech is Shakespeare's farewell to the theatre.

Which pierces so, that it assaults
Mercy itself, and frees all faults.
As you from crimes would pardoned be,   335
Let your indulgence set me free.

Exit

Exploring Act 5

Prospero, 2009

Activity 1: Prospero's stories

a. In pairs, look back at Prospero's speech in lines 25–32 on page 155. Read the lines aloud together and then agree a paraphrase of them. What do you think Prospero is saying about vengeance and forgiveness in these lines?

b. Now look at Prospero's speech in lines 298–309 on pages 173–175. Read these lines aloud together and then agree a paraphrase of them. To what extent do you think Prospero has forgiven the nobles?

c. Discuss what you think Prospero will reveal to the nobles and what he will keep secret. How much do you think he will reveal about his magical powers and about Ariel? How much do you think he will admit about how he has controlled their lives since they arrived on the island?

d. Discuss how you think the nobles will respond. How might they feel if Prospero tells them everything he has done and the power he has? How responsible do they feel for the life Prospero and Miranda have lived?

e. Using the ideas you shared in tasks a–d, write a script for an additional short scene, Act 5 Scene 2, which is set in Prospero's cell later that evening. Include:

- Prospero's summary of how he and Miranda came to the island and survived living there
- what Prospero chooses to tell the nobles about what has happened to them since they arrived on the island
- questions and comments from the nobles
- clues for the audience about how much the characters have forgiven each other and how much they still want revenge.

Prospero, 2016

Activity 2: The *Milan Herald*

In groups, discuss what the citizens of Milan might think about:

- the political drama of Prospero returning to power, replacing Antonio as their leader
- the love story of the upcoming royal wedding of Miranda to the Prince of Naples
- the strange stories the crew and passengers of the ship tell about their adventures in foreign lands.

One of you should take on the role of editor of the local Milan newspaper, while the others are journalists on your team. Together, create the centre spread of the paper, which focuses exclusively on stories connected to the issues above. The editor is responsible for how the pages look, for ensuring there is a good balance of facts, opinions, interviews and images, and for writing the newspaper's editorial comments on the story. You could include:

- **vox pops** from citizens who remember life under Prospero's rule 12 years ago
- speculation about how Miranda is adjusting to life as a celebrity
- an interview with the Boatswain or with Trinculo about the strange island.

Key term

Vox pop comment or opinion from a member of the public

Exploring the play

Caliban and spirits, 2009

Activity 1: Understanding the activities

a. In groups, discuss what might have happened to the characters in the play five years on. Are Miranda and Ferdinand still happily married? Has Prospero given up all his magic? Where is Caliban now and is he happy?

b. Miranda first arrived on the island when she was 3 and left 12 years later. Imagine she is now 21 and she is returning to the island. How might she feel? What might she find?

c. In your groups, one of you should take on the role of an interviewer, while the others take the roles of Miranda, Caliban and Ferdinand. The interviewer is responsible for asking the characters questions focusing on Miranda's return to the island. The questions could refer to memories of key events and places on the island, emotions towards the other characters, how this has affected their lives and how it feels to return to the same place and people.

d. Write a report of what the interviewer has uncovered together with a summary of what you think will happen next.

Ferdinand and Miranda, 2016

Activity 2: Assessing the relevance of the play

The Tempest is one of the most produced plays in the world. Productions are often in modern dress and can reflect many aspects of different cultures from around the world. The RSC production in 2009, for example, was performed by a South African company in the context of South African culture and traditions, and the 2006 production was set in the context of Inuit culture.

a. Look back at the photos on pages 20, 90, 124 and 136 in this book, and discuss how you think the directors use costume and setting to connect the world of the play with our world today.
b. Discuss the following questions:
   - In what ways are Miranda and Ferdinand like young people today and in what ways are they not?
   - Do any of the ways Stephano and Trinculo, and Sebastian and Antonio, behave remind you of how people behave today?
c. Why do you think *The Tempest* is considered to be worth studying in this day and age? Following your discussion, write an essay with the title 'How is Shakespeare's play *The Tempest* still relevant today?' Use the questions above to help structure your essay. Include key moments and quotations from the script to support your ideas.

Shakespeare's life

William Shakespeare is probably the most famous playwright of all time. Here's a summary of his life, his work and important events at the time.

1564
William Shakespeare is born in Stratford-upon-Avon.

1595
Romeo and Juliet and *A Midsummer Night's Dream* first performed.

1593
Shakespeare's first published work, the poem *Venus and Adonis*.

1592–3
The London theatres close for several months because of a plague outbreak.

1596
The Merchant of Venice first performed.

1596
Hamnet Shakespeare dies and is buried in Stratford-upon-Avon.

1597
Shakespeare buys a large house, New Place, in Stratford-upon-Avon.

1608
Death of Shakespeare's mother, Mary.

1606
Macbeth first performed.

1605
The Gunpowder Plot, a threat to blow up the king in Parliament, fails. ➤

1611
The Tempest first performed.

1611
The *King James Bible*, or *Authorized Version*, is published.

1613
Shakespeare's last plays, *The Two Noble Kinsmen* and *Henry VIII*, both jointly written with John Fletcher, are performed.

1582

He marries Anne Hathaway.

1583

Susanna Shakespeare, William and Anne's first child, is born.

1585

Two more children, the twins Hamnet and Judith, are born.

1592

By this date Shakespeare had begun his career in London as an actor and playwright. A rival, Robert Greene, described him in print as an 'upstart crow'.

1588

◁ Spanish Armada is defeated.

1598

Much Ado About Nothing first performed.

1599

Shakespeare's theatre company builds the Globe theatre in London. ➤

1603

Death of Queen Elizabeth. The new king, James I, takes over the patronage of Shakespeare's company and they are renamed the King's Men.

1601

Death of Shakespeare's father, John.

1616

Shakespeare dies in Stratford-upon-Avon and is buried in a local church.

1623

The first collected edition of his plays, the *First Folio*, is published in London. ➤

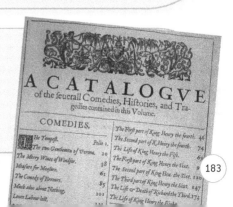

Shakespeare's language

Shakespeare's language can be difficult for us to understand for two different reasons. One is historical: words and their meanings, and the ways people express themselves, have changed over the four hundred years since he wrote. The other is poetic: Shakespeare's characters don't speak how ordinary people, even in the Jacobean period, would have spoken. They speak in a heightened, poetic language full of repetition and elaboration.

Verse and prose

Most Shakespeare plays are written in verse with a small proportion of prose included. You can tell verse from prose on the page because verse lines are usually shorter and each line begins with a capital letter, whereas prose lines usually begin with lower-case letters (unless it is the beginning of a sentence) and continue to the very edge of the paper. Verse is a more formal way of speaking and is often associated with higher-status characters, whereas servants or other lower-class figures more often speak prose. Comic scenes are sometimes in prose, where the language is more relaxed and natural.

Sebastian, Ariel and Antonio, 2006

Shakespeare's verse is often called blank verse – blank means it does not rhyme. But occasionally he does use rhyme, sometimes in a couplet (two rhyming lines) at the end of a scene to signal that it has come to a conclusion. For example, here's Ariel's couplet that concludes Act 2 Scene 1 in which he protects the sleeping King Alonso from his brother:

Ariel	Prospero, my lord, shall know what I have done. So, king, go safely on to seek thy son.

At other times, Shakespeare uses rhyme to suggest formality. In the masque scene (Act 4 Scene 1) of *The Tempest*, for instance, the goddesses speak in a regular rhyming verse to distinguish this magical performance from the speech rhythms of the rest of the play (see the top of page 185).

Hail, many-coloured messenger, that ne'er
Dost disobey the wife of Jupiter;
Who, with thy saffron wings, upon my flowers
Diffusest honey drops, refreshing showers

Iambic pentameter

Poetry – like music – is words ordered into rhythm. The metre of poetry is like its drumbeat. Most of Shakespeare's verse lines are written in iambic pentameter. A pentameter means that there are five beats to the line (and usually ten syllables); iambic means that the beats are alternately weak and strong, or unstressed and stressed.

An example from *The Tempest* is Prospero's speech at the beginning of Act 5 Scene 1 when he appears in his magic robes to bring the plot to an end (see below). The numbers below the line count the syllables; the marks below that show that the syllables alternate between unstressed (signalled with -) and stressed (/). It looks more complicated when you write it down than when you read it aloud.

Prospero   Now does my project gather to a head.

            1   2   3 4 5 6 7 8 9 10

          -     /   - / - / - / - /

As with music, the sound of Shakespeare's language would get repetitive if he never varied the rhythm. So sometimes he changes the arrangement of stressed and unstressed syllables, and sometimes lines can be read with different emphases, depending on the actor's interpretation. Reading Shakespeare's lines aloud often helps.

One clue: often Shakespeare puts important words or ideas at the end of his lines, rather than at the beginning. If you look down a speech and look at the last word in each line you can usually get some idea of the main point of the speech. One additional clue: with longer speeches, often the beginning and the end are the most important, and the middle says the same thing in different ways.

Shakespeare's world

Knowing something about life in Shakespeare's England is often helpful for our understanding of his plots and characters, and of the assumptions that members of his audiences would have had when they went to see his plays. But it is also important to remember that he was an imaginative playwright, making up stories for entertainment.

Just as we wouldn't necessarily rely on modern Hollywood films or television drama to depict our everyday reality, so too we need sometimes to acknowledge that Shakespeare is showing his audiences something exotic, unfamiliar or fairy tale.

London

At some point in his early twenties, Shakespeare moved from the country town of Stratford to London. Thousands of people at the time did the same, moving to the city for work and other opportunities, and London expanded rapidly during the Elizabethan and Jacobean periods. It was a busy, commercial place that had outgrown the original walled city and was now organised around the main thoroughfare, the river Thames. Shakespeare never sets a play in contemporary London, although many of his urban locations, particularly Venice, seem to recall the inns and streets and bustle of the city in which he and his audiences lived and worked.

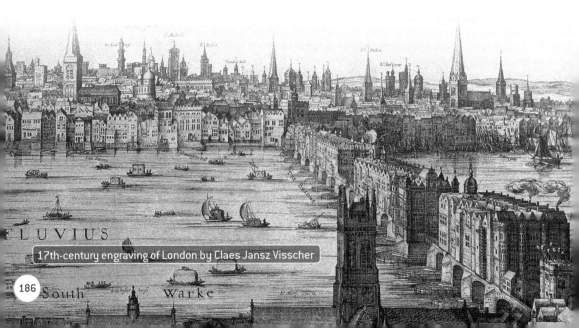

17th-century engraving of London by Claes Jansz Visscher

As a port city, London was a place where people from different places mixed together, although its society was much less racially diverse than now. Jews had been banned from England in the medieval period, although there were some secret communities in London, so almost no one in Shakespeare's England would ever have met a Jewish person. A visit of Arab ambassadors from North Africa to Queen Elizabeth's court in 1600 must have seemed very exotic indeed.

Kingship and succession

Early modern societies were not democratic. Ruling families tended to pass power between them, as we see in *The Tempest*. The play was written under the reign of James I, who wrote a number of books about the ways in which kingly authority was directly given by God. The idea of regicide – or killing a king – as Antonio suggests to Sebastian in Act 2 Scene 1, would have been shocking to audiences.

A king's group of advisors and servants would travel with him. Often a king paid a jester to sing or tell jokes at court.

King James I was the King of England from 1603–1625

187

Shakespeare's company and the theatre

When he wrote *The Tempest*, Shakespeare was an actor, the chief playwright and an investor in a company of actors sponsored by King James and known as the King's Men. The company performed their plays in the Globe theatre on the banks of the river Thames in London. The Globe was an open-air theatre with a large yard for standing audience members and tiered seating around the outside. The King's Men also had an indoor theatre called Blackfriars, which was more expensive to attend and had better technical effects: Shakespeare may be drawing on these when he includes pieces of stage business such as Ariel descending from above the stage like a harpy (a mythological creature with a bird's body and a female face).

The 'Flower' portrait of Shakespeare, c. 1830

As King James's preferred acting troupe, Shakespeare's company also performed at court and there they experienced a different form of dramatic entertainment called the masque. Jacobean masques were very over-the-top and expensive shows of wealth and power; the masques were full of grand costumes, music, dancing and purpose-built staging, with some highly technical effects. A famous architect, Inigo Jones, often designed complex scenery for these masques; he believed that the audience's enjoyment of the masque was more for its visual splendour than for its words. Jones developed techniques including machines to lower and raise actors so that they looked as if they were flying, which also may have influenced Shakespeare when he created the character of Ariel. Masque technology was a bit like modern cinema special effects: full of hi-tech visual surprise.

Back in the regular theatre, Shakespeare's acting troupe, the King's Men, was probably about twelve or fourteen men (male actors played all the roles, including female ones), so they also doubled up and played more than one part. It is likely that most costumes were the Jacobean equivalent of 'modern dress': so that actors were wearing clothes similar to those around the audience and the London streets. Audiences needed to bring their imaginations with them to the theatre.

The audience for Shakespeare's plays was quite mixed, but probably tended to be younger rather than older and male rather than female. Entry to the open-air theatres like the Globe was cheap — one penny, the cost of two pints of beer — so a relatively diverse social mix could attend; for the Blackfriars it was more expensive and more exclusive. We don't know how well educated the audience was, although educational opportunities were expanding during the sixteenth and seventeenth centuries and historians think that male literacy levels in London at this point may have been as high as 50%. Literacy was connected to social status: wealthier individuals were much more likely to be educated than poorer ones. But more people went to see Shakespeare's plays in the theatre than read them when they were printed.

The modern Globe Theatre in London is modelled on the theatre that Shakespeare's company built in 1599

Shakespeare's sources

Shakespeare read lots of different works that had a direct or indirect influence on his plays. Often we can identify one major source that he used for the plot and characters, but not in the case of *The Tempest*. We do know that Shakespeare was inspired by the recently published eyewitness account of a real-life shipwreck at Bermuda. We also know that Gonzalo's long speech about his ideal society is taken from the works of a French philosopher called Montaigne, who also influenced other Shakespeare plays. In the speech in which Prospero gives up his magic, which begins 'You elves of hills, brooks, standing lakes and groves' (Act 5 Scene 1), Shakespeare returns to one of his favourite books, the Latin poet Ovid's *Metamorphoses*. In Metamorphoses, this speech is given to the sorceress Medea.

Viola, Twelfth Night, 2012

The Tempest comes towards the end of Shakespeare's career. Lots of readers of the play have suggested that Prospero might be a self-portrait of Shakespeare, whose literary 'magic' on the stage is much like Prospero's control of the characters on his island. Shakespeare seems to use a number of his own previous plays as source material here too: in his history plays, he showed family rivalries (conflicts) in politics: in *Hamlet* we see one brother seizing power from another brother, much like the back-story in *The Tempest*. In *A Midsummer Night's Dream*, Shakespeare explores the magical world and lots of his comedies end with young lovers marrying, as they do here.

The supernatural

Ideas of magic in Shakespeare's time were not completely separate from ideas about new science and learning. The real-life Elizabethan magician John Dee, who some people believe was a model for Shakespeare's Prospero, worked for Queen Elizabeth as a pioneer of astronomy (the study of the stars and the universe) and navigation, as well as conjuring up spirits and believing in magic. Like Dee's library, Prospero's books probably include lots of academic titles as well as books of spells.

Just as in modern magical stories such as the *Lord of the Rings* or the *Harry Potter* books, in early modern stories, the good magician was often contrasted with the dark or evil sorcerer. Indeed, Prospero compares himself to Caliban's mother, Sycorax, in the play and suggests that he uses his magic for good, whereas she was a 'witch': opinions vary about whether Prospero's own motives are as harmless as he suggests.

People in the Jacobean period had many different views about the forces ruling their world, including the position of supernatural elements. Like now, they might enjoy fictional magical tales in the theatre, even though they accepted that they were not true in the real world.

A spirit, The Tempest, 2006

Exploration and the New World

The first European explorers of the so-called New World (the continent of the Americas) arrived 100 years before Shakespeare's time. In the time of King James, an English settlement called Jamestown was temporarily established in Virginia. In this community, the English settlers needed the help of the native people for survival.

Travel to the New World was very difficult and dangerous: the journey by wooden sailing ship across the Atlantic Ocean took many weeks, and shipwrecks and storms were frequent. The word 'hurricane', meaning a powerful tempest or storm, came into the English language in the sixteenth century (from Spanish) to describe these new experiences.

'The Tempest', Act I Scene I, the Shipwreck, 1793, oil on canvas by Philippe Jacques de Loutherbourg

Attitudes to the New World were inconsistent. On the one hand, it was seen as a lush, empty country where settlers could make their fortune, and the source of new foodstuffs such as the potato and tobacco, both of which arrived in England from Virginia in the sixteenth century. On the other hand, there was a fear that the native people of the New World were backward or perhaps not even fully human, that there were monsters or cannibals or other dangerous creatures that would threaten European travellers. To some people, the New World seemed like a different place with different ideas and perhaps offered the possibility of a fairer human society; for others, it was like a place caught in the past – less developed than Europe. These contradictory attitudes were a bit like twentieth-century ideas about space travel: some stories about space travel emphasise the new possibilities of the unexplored; others are full of fear about alien threat.

It was common for explorers to travel to unfamiliar places to bring back human or animal souvenirs: a few years after *The Tempest*, the young Native American woman Pocahontas came to London with her English husband and fascinated King James and his court. Other expeditions brought back polar bears and other animals.

The Bear Interlude, The Merry Wives of Windsor, 1955

193

Marriage and courtship

Elizabethan and Jacobean marriages tended to be seen as alliances between families, as much as between the couple themselves. In part, Prospero is keen to bring Miranda and Ferdinand together to secure his return to Milan in alliance with Ferdinand's father, Alonso. In wealthy or noble families, a suitable marriage arranged between the parents of the couple was common and the couple themselves might spend little or no time together before being married; for ordinary people, there may have been more possibility to choose a partner, although parental permission was still important. Marriage was a practical commitment rather than, or as well as, a romantic partnership: perhaps couples then did not place such high emotional expectations on their married relationships as in modern western societies. Some high-born people might be engaged as children, but the age of consent was 21 (Shakespeare needed his father's permission to marry aged just 18). Most Jacobean brides and grooms were in their mid-twenties when they married.

Sexual morality was different for men and for women: for men – as for Ferdinand – sexual experience was socially acceptable, but for women, to lose their virginity outside of marriage was to lose their social value. Prospero is deeply concerned that Ferdinand and Miranda should not sleep together before their marriage is formally conducted.

Rose Oatley, Sir Hugh Lacy and Rowland Lacy, *The Shoemaker's Holiday*, 2014

Weddings could happen in church, but they also could be legally contracted if the couple promised to marry each other in front of a witness and then consummated their relationship. A betrothal or engagement might precede the formal marriage service: this was a legally binding commitment between the couple. The Jacobean church marriage service suggested that marriage had three purposes: children, the avoidance of fornication, and the comfort and companionship between husband and wife. Bible verses in the service instructed husbands to love and cherish their wives, and wives to submit to their husband's authority. The couple would wear their best clothes (the tradition of a bride wearing white came later) and afterwards there would usually be feasting.

Lysander, Hermia, Helena and Demetrius, *A Midsummer Night's Dream*, 2005

Marriages were subject to the same problems and stresses then as now, although there was almost no divorce allowed in the Jacobean period. Cheating on your husband or wife, or being married to more than one person were seen as sins to be punished by the church courts; a clergyman who broke the rules on the correct forms of marriage would also be in serious trouble. A man whose wife was unfaithful, or rumoured to be unfaithful, was ridiculed and disrespected. He was known as a 'cuckold' and it was said that horns grew on his head.

Illegitimate children were often acknowledged within noble families — they were thought to have dark and negative personalities because they were born outside of marriage, which was considered immoral — but poor women who gave birth outside marriage were often left homeless and penniless. Lower-status women were the most vulnerable in Shakespeare's England: if a woman was thrown out by her family her prospects were very harsh indeed.

Women

Ideas about the ideal woman are current in many societies, including modern ones. Just as we know that most real women now do not conform to the thin, beautiful, youthful ideal of modern advertising, so too probably Jacobean women were different from the models given to them in conduct books, sermons and literature. The ideal woman, according to writers on morality in Shakespeare's England, remained meekly at home. She was chaste, honest, silent and obedient to her husband's will.

A moral double standard meant that women's behaviour, especially their chastity, was much more policed than that of men. Unmarried women were expected to obey their fathers and conduct themselves modestly. Women did not attend school or university, although wealthy ones might be educated at home. Except for widows, women could not hold property in their own right. But alongside these stereotypes there were many exceptional women, from Queen Elizabeth to the writer Mary Sidney and the pirate Mary Killigrew, as well as ordinary women living, working and running their households.

Bianca, *Love's Sacrifice*, 2015

Children

In the Jacobean period, children were expected to obey their parents; wives their husbands; servants their masters. Consequences of disobedience could be very serious. Children in higher-class families often lived with relatives or were quite distant from their parents; for lower-status families, young children would be expected to work in the household. It is likely that the young Shakespeare would have helped out in his father's workshop. Young children in noble families wore the same clothes for both sexes until a ceremony called 'breeching' when boys began to wear breeches (trousers), aged about 7.

Falstaff's Page and Doll Tearsheet, Henry IV Part 2, 2014

Key terms glossary

Adjective a word that describes a noun, e.g. blue, happy, big

Adverb a word that describes a verb, e.g. quickly

Alliteration words that begin with the same sound

Aside when a character addresses a remark to the audience, or to another character, that other characters on the stage do not hear

Atmosphere the mood created by staging choices

Back-story what happened to any of the characters before the start of the play

Casting deciding which actors should play which roles

Clown an actor skilled in comedy and improvisation who could often sing and dance as well

Dialogue a discussion between two or more people

Dramatic irony when the audience knows something that some characters in the play do not

Emphasis stress given to words when speaking

Extended metaphor describing something by comparing it to something else over several lines

Freeze-frame a physical, still image created by people to represent an object, place, person or feeling

Gesture a movement, often using the hands or head, to express a feeling or idea

Iambic pentameter the rhythm Shakespeare uses to write his plays. Each line in this rhythm contains approximately ten syllables. 'Iambic' means putting the stress on the second syllable of each beat. 'Pentameter' means five beats with two syllables in each beat

Imagery visually descriptive language

Improvise make up in the moment

Infer form an opinion based on evidence

Metaphor describing something by comparing it with something else

Monologue a long speech in which a character expresses their thoughts. Other characters may be present

Objective what a character wants to get or achieve in a scene

Pace the speed at which someone speaks

Paraphrase a line or section of text expressed in your own words

Personification giving an object or concept human qualities

Plot the events of a story

Prop an object used in the play, e.g. a dagger

Quatrain a stanza of four lines

Shared lines lines of iambic pentameter shared between characters. This implies a closeness between them in some way

Simile a comparison that uses the words 'like' or 'as'

Soliloquy a speech in which a character is alone on stage and expresses their thoughts and feelings aloud to the audience

Stage direction an instruction in the text of a play, e.g. indicating which characters enter and exit a scene

Staging the process of selecting, adapting and developing the stage space in which a play will be performed

Subplot a minor plot often reflecting themes of the main plot

Syllable part of a word that is one sound, e.g. 'tempest' has two syllables 'tem' and 'pest'

Tactics the methods a character uses to get what they want

Theme the main ideas explored in a piece of literature, e.g. the themes of power and authority, hope and fear, family, vengeance and forgiveness might be considered key themes of The Tempest

Tone as in 'tone of voice'; expressing an attitude through how you say something

Unit of action one moment, or 'beat' of something happening, which can be described in one sentence

Verb a word describing an action or a state, e.g. jump, shout, believe, exist

Vox pop comment or opinion from a member of the public